Governor's Travels

How I Left Politics, Learned to Back Up a Bus, and Found America

Happy travels!

by **Angus King,**
former Governor of Maine

Angus King

Down East

Design by Lynda Chilton

ISBN 978-0-89272-973-9
Printed in the United States of America
5 4 3 2 1

Down East
BOOKS·MAGAZINE·ONLINE
www.downeast.com

Distributed to the trade by
National Book Network

Library of Congress Catalog Information
available upon request

Contents

Introduction

I t was about eight o'clock on a cold January night when the state trooper drove away and I was alone for the first time in eight years.

A few minutes before, I had been Governor of Maine, with all that entailed—staff, special parking (pretty much the best part of the job), constant attention from the press, standing ovations (sometimes, at least in the first few years), and 24-hour-a-day supervision by the state police. But in one of those delightful turnings of our democratic system, the moment my successor took the oath, I was out, and the whole thing disappeared with the receding taillights of the trooper's car.

Transitions in business are usually gradual (assuming they're voluntary), and power and its accoutrements sort of ooze from the old leader to the new. Not so in politics. One day you're The Man, and the next you're simply *a* man—and your chief function is to bear the blame for whatever goes wrong that your successor has to cope with in the first couple of years.

I understand that this cold-turkey transition can be hard. They say Lyndon Johnson never recovered from being President—and died from a kind of emptiness soon after his political life was over. I even had a consultant contact me toward the end of my term offering special counseling on Life After High Office. Standing there on that January night did feel a

little strange—there was regret, sure, but regret tinged by relief to be free of the intense burden that is part of any such job.

But those emotions came and went in a matter of minutes, partly as a result of the way I had approached the job from the beginning and partly as a result of the plan we (my wife, Mary, and I) had made for this moment.

My approach to the job can be summed up pretty simply—I never viewed politics as a career. Important, yes; worthy of intense commitment, of course—but it was not my whole life. I came to active politics late in life (I was 49 when I declared for Governor—and had never run for public office) and had already had a full life, including two marriages, four kids, a law practice, a business start-up, fifteen years as a TV talk show host, and a bout with cancer. I saw politics as a way to make a contribution and satisfy my penchant for public policy, but not as something I couldn't live without.

This approach had all kinds of good consequences, starting with the campaign and continuing right up to the night I left office. Essentially, it liberated me from the tyranny of *needing* the job; I was free to be myself (very handy in a campaign) and to try to do whatever I thought was right in any given situation (equally handy while in office). It led me to be one of the only two independent governors in the country in the late nineties (Quiz: who was the other?)* And if I had to put my political philosophy on a bumper sticker, it would be something like "I call 'em as I see 'em."

I always had a kind of Myth of Cincinatus idea about politics—that public service was something you do for a while in between stints at real life. And when your time is up, you return to the plow, which is hopefully still somewhere close to where you left it.

The other thing that made that moment manageable was that I had to get home to check on overpass heights between Williamsburg, Virginia, and Cape Hatteras, on the Outer Banks of North Carolina. And this brings me to The Plan, the realization of which is the subject of this book.

Neither Mary nor I can remember who first thought of taking the kids out of school and heading off on a prolonged RV trip around the country when I left office, but we know when it moved from the realm of idea to that of plan. In the spring of 1999, we had decided to do a trial run and, during school vacation, flew to Phoenix, rented an RV for a week, and explored Arizona. It was somewhere on the drive from Phoenix to Sedona (I put it right

I always [thought] that public service was something you do for a while between stints at real life.

around the charming and somewhat eccentric town of Jerome) that we realized this just might work.

We learned a couple of things on that trip (besides that we liked the freedom and spontaneity of the RV lifestyle): that you need to tow a car, for example; and if you're going to spend a substantial amount of time together in such a vehicle (or any time whatsoever if it's raining), the bigger the vehicle, the better.

So, the next morning that January—about twelve hours after the trooper dropped me off—we were on the road, headed south with no particular destination but with a very clear intention: to discover America, ourselves, and a little something about family. What follows is the story of that trip— part travelogue, part executive transition manual, part celebration. It's more impressionist than comprehensive, but the idea is to convey the feel and fun of our journey.

But there's a subversive intent as well—to make you want to go, too. See you on the road!

Angus King

Angus King
Brunswick, Maine
Spring 2011

* My good friend and inveterate tweaker of the political establishment, Jesse Ventura.

HOW TO CHOOSE THE RIGHT RV

One of the wonderful things about capitalism is that it will, by and large, spit out products in a bewildering variety of style, design, functionality, and price, as long as there are at least a few people out there likely to buy them. (How else, for example, do you explain the Pontiac Aztec?)

This certainly applies in the world of RVs. There are units that drop into the bed of a pick-up, trailers in all shapes and sizes—from pop-ups to grand "fifth wheels" (the large trailers that don't hook on a trailer hitch but attach to the truck via a kind of

foot mounted in the middle of the pick-up bed), and everything in between. In this category, of course, is the classic Airstream, whose aerodynamic polished aluminum bodies have been a fixture on American highways for almost eighty years.

So you have some basic decisions to make before you start looking in earnest.

The first choice is between self-contained and a trailer. The advantage of a trailer is that you can get where you're going—the Shady Dell in Bisbee, Arizona, for example—unhook the trailer, and then use the untethered truck or SUV to explore the surroundings. The other side of the coin is that if you choose one of the self-contained units, unless it's pretty small, you'll have to tow a car. We learned this on our practice trip in Arizona. Once you get one of these rigs (which is the cool RV term for

your unit, as in, "Nice rig; what kind of mileage you gettin'?") parked, plugged in, and leveled, you don't want to have to undo everything to take the kids downtown to the copper mine exhibit or pick up a quart of milk.

So either way, you'll be towing—either a car behind the RV or an RV behind the car (or truck)—unless of course you opt for one of the smaller self-contained units ("Class Bs") that are more like big vans or small RVs. But don't worry, towing is no big deal.

Here are the basic categories of self-contained units (i.e., engine and living space all in one): Class As are the big bus-type vehicles like our Dutch Star; Class Bs are smaller conversion-van types, and Class Cs (which are mostly what you see on the road) are a truck chassis with a boxy living unit that has a protrusion extending over the roof of the truck cab. Class Bs are generally smaller than Class C's, so it can be a little confusing.

These units come in lengths from around 20 feet up to 45 feet, but the most common sizes are between 30 and 40 feet.

In deciding which way to go (in this case, literally), the first question is how many people will be going and how long will you be on the road. The more people and the longer the trip, the bigger the rig should be.

A lot of people make the mistake of starting out too small because they are intimidated by the idea of driving a bus. My experience was that once you get above 20 feet or so (the size of a big SUV), it doesn't really matter—the back of the thing will go wherever you go, it'll just take a little longer to get there. We met a lot of folks who had "started out" in a 34-footer, for example, only to find after a few weeks on the road that driving it was no problem and they wished they had gone for more space.

Speaking of space, you can't have too many slide-outs. These are wonderful room expanders that pop out from the sides of the rig once you have parked. They expand and retract at the push of a button, literally making the bus wider, and they can add a huge amount of comfort to your experience. For a while, two slides was cool, but in 2002 and after, the manufacturers started making them with three (what we had on the Dutch Star) or even four. Again, if you're going to be on the road for more than weekends or a few weeks, and especially if there are more than two of you, go for as many slide-outs as you can afford.

Next, you have to decide about engine type—gas or diesel. This is almost purely a question of price; if you can swing it, diesel is generally better. It's more powerful (a big deal when you're struggling up a mountain road), more economical, and more dependable. The purchase price for a diesel RV is usually about 25% higher than a gas model, but it's generally worth it.

A "diesel pusher" is especially desirable because the engine is in the back—about 35 feet behind the driver—which makes it super quiet up front.

Another question is whether to buy new or used. The downside of new is that you pay top dollar and lose the depreciation the minute you drive it off the lot. On the other hand, when you go for new, you can get just what you want, with a warranty, and you know somebody before you didn't drive it 100,000 miles without changing the oil. We intended to buy used, but couldn't find exactly what we were looking for (accommodations for the kids—pretty unusual in the RV world, which is mostly geared to retirees) and decided to take our chances with the depreciation.

I think we made the right decision. We sold our rig after a year of use and 15,000 miles for about 85% of what we paid for it. On the other hand, our buyer got a great deal—the right rig (they had kids, too) that was really just broken in (15,000 miles is nothing on a diesel). Study the Web—and if you find what you're looking for at the right price, go for it; but if nothing appeals to you, buy new; there's nothing like the smell of a new vehicle.

Getting Started
The Family, the Vehicle, and the Maiden Voyage

1

It turns out that our kids were the perfect ages for the trip. Ben was twelve when we left, which was just young enough to be willing to go at all and just shy of the angst that comes with teenagerhood. Molly, on the other hand, was nine and old enough to take it all in. If Ben had been even a year older, I doubt we could have gotten him on the road at all, if Molly had been a year or two younger, she wouldn't have appreciated everything we saw and experienced.

Of course, this doesn't mean they were enthusiastic; it was our idea, after all. But at least they were willing to give it a try, and by the time we got about a hundred miles from home, the die was cast—it was too far for them to walk back.

Actually, a crucial moment had come—somewhat by accident—several months before, on the day our RV was delivered to our dealer, Mountain Road RV in Sabattus, Maine. We were at home when we got the call that it was in and that we could come over and check her out. By chance, both kids had friends visiting at the time and so we scooped everyone up—seven or eight kids in all—and took two cars full for our first look at what would be our home on the road.

> *Our maiden voyage was one of those experiences that you look back upon in wonder: I must have been nuts; we're lucky to be alive.*

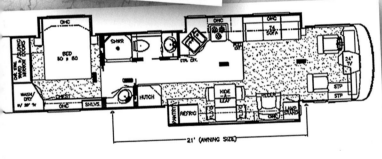

2003 Dutch Star Diesel Pusher 4006

And there she was in all her forty-foot glory—she looked plenty cool to me but I wasn't so sure about the kids. I needn't have worried, though. Before Ben or Molly could say a word, their friends pronounced immediate judgment—"Wow, this is awesome; you guys are really lucky! Can we go on the trip, too?"

That's all it took; sometimes peer pressure can be a wonderful thing.

We looked for the right RV for at least two years before settling on the Newmar Dutch Star (looking, by the way, is a big part of the fun). We visited dealers all over Maine and anywhere else we happened to be, subscribed to RV magazines, and talked to friends who had RV experience—but the real looking occurred on the Web.

Searching eBay and RVsearch.com became my late-night recreation after long days of Doing the People's Business (and they were long days). I would read the specs, enlarge the pictures, visit chat rooms, read reviews, and google promising leads. (I don't know about you, but I feel kind of proud that I was present when a new verb—to google—was invented. Imagine being around when someone came up with "run" or "jump.")

And the Web is an amazing resource. It approaches the economists' ideal of a perfect market, where buyers and sellers have almost total access to one another and information is unlimited, available, and easily accessible. We are barely beginning to realize the potential this has for fundamental social, cultural, and eco-nomic change—but that's another book (and Tom Friedman has already written it).

Once we settled on the type of RV and the most popular brands, it was the owner reviews I found most useful. Salesmen and company brochures can paint glowing pictures of power and comfort, but it's the guy who's paid out the cash and driven one across the Rockies a couple of times who can give you the best idea of what you're getting into.

Our maiden voyage was one of those experiences that you look back upon in wonder: I must have been nuts; we're lucky to be alive.

Here's how it happened.

It was Mary who had the truly good idea that leaving Maine in mid-January in a forty-foot bus during a howling snowstorm might not be the best way to start our trip. So the obvious solution was to move the bus south before the snow flew, drive the first leg out of Maine, with the family in the car, and start off in the balmy weather sure to be found in Virginia and the Carolinas that time of year (little did we know . . . but more on that later). This turned out to be a great plan, but not for any of the reasons we thought.

The real reason it was a good idea is the "Things Will Go Wrong on Your First Trip" rule, and you don't want to be screwing up while your spouse and kids just sit there watching and offering helpful comments.

So on Friday the first weekend in November, State Trooper Bob Slattery (he had apparently drawn the short straw) and I headed the Dutch Star out from Brunswick, Maine, to Williamsburg, Virginia. I should have realized that it might not be the most auspicious beginning when I opened the

door—literally to start the drive—and noticed the front tire was flat. Really flat, as in not drivable. And you can't just whip out the jack and change a tire on a forty-foot bus.

The rig had been in our front yard ("dooryard" in Maine parlance) for a month or so while we packed it up in preparation for the trip. (It also served as a movie theater for the kids and their friends and was a great conversation piece in the neighborhood.) Somehow during this period, the right front tire had slowly deflated, but not enough to be noticeable until the day we were to leave. Here was the problem: there was no way we could change the tire—it would have to be handled by a shop capable of dealing with truck tires—but there was also no way we could drive it to such a shop, even one nearby.

The solution was the first in a series of revelations that turned my admiration for the Dutch Star into full-fledged love. I love products that are intuitive, that are designed in a way that make you think the designers have read your mind. You say to yourself, "Wouldn't it be cool if it could do X, Y, or Z," and you quickly find out that it does—that they've anticipated your question, and answered it. Probably the Apple Macintosh is the best example of this kind of intuitive design around today (Microsoft Windows, on the other hand, not so much—how intuitive is it to click "start" when you want to shut down?).

In the case of the Dutch Star, the designers had added a takeoff valve to the hydraulic air-pressure system (which feeds pressurized air to the suspension) so you could snap on an air hose and blow up your tires! How cool is that?

So we ran to the nearby auto parts store, bought a fifty-foot air hose, inflated the tire enough to make it drivable, and headed cautiously to the tire dealer. They quickly figured out the problem was a faulty valve and fixed it in twenty minutes. (This would be the only tire problem we'd have for the whole trip.) Not exactly a triumphant leave-taking, but it worked, and Bob and I had the satisfaction of having overcome our first crisis. Unfortunately, there would be more.

The first leg—from Maine, through New Hampshire and Massachusetts, and into Connecticut—was uneventful. I began to get the feel of the bus—how it accelerated, turned, and stopped. I was also learning how much fun it could be to drive, and how easy, once you got over the initial feeling that you were maneuvering an elephant down the highway.

So getting into Connecticut was no problem. The problem was getting out. For eight years the Maine State Police had looked after me very well, particularly when it came to getting from place to place. They were masters of logistics and directions. Want the best route to eastern Maine in a snowstorm? These guys know every fork in the road, as well as when the plows are likely to come by. So when our directions for this trip—nicely printed out in duplicate—said take various interstates south to the Merritt Parkway, then south to the New York Throughway and the Tappan Zee Bridge, well, that's what we did. Unfortunately.

As we pulled onto the Merrit Parkway, the warning signs were all around us. First, a guy went by beeping his horn like crazy. "Hey," I said, "must be from Maine. Probably recognized me." The ego of the politician at work obscuring the real facts. Next, we noticed that the bridges seemed to

The warning signs were all around us. First, a guy went by beeping his horn like crazy. "Hey," I said, "must be from Maine. Probably recognized me." Next, we noticed that the bridges seemed to be getting lower and lower.

be getting lower and lower. Eventually we had to go under the arched bridges in the middle because the clearance on the sides was uncomfortably close.

Then we passed a stopped highway patrolman who immediately hit his siren as we blew by. "Must be after a speeder," I offered. (At least I didn't use the "probably recognized me" line again.) Oh, and I should probably mention that by this time night was falling and it was starting to rain.

Somewhere during all this, we passed a sign that read, "Low Bridge Ahead—Clearance 9 Feet." (The Dutch Star was 12' 6", by the way.) "What do you make of that, Bob?" I asked, mild concern creeping into my voice.

"No problem, sir," Bob replied. (Remember, I was still in office at this point and was therefore still The Man, thus the "sir.") "That's probably a bridge on one of the feeder roads after you leave the highway."

"OK," I said, not so sure.

Then came another sign, this one bright orange: "Caution—Next Bridge 9 Feet."

"What do you think, Bob?" my voice rising.

"GET OFF," Bob shouted, and I headed for the exit with barely time to signal and no idea what we would find at the bottom of the ramp. We pulled into a parking lot just off the highway to figure our next move (and to take a deep breath, if the truth be known), when the trooper we had passed several miles back flew by on the highway above us with his siren on and all lights flashing. Then we both knew—he was looking for us.

At that point, we had basically two options—stay off the highway and wind through the wilds of suburban Connecticut in a twelve-and-a-half-foot-high, forty-foot-long bus in the dark and rain and try to find our way to a real highway, or return the way we had come and take the spur back to I-95 we noticed when we got on the Parkway. By now we realized that going back on the Parkway was completely illegal. But we also realized that we *could* make it back in about twenty minutes (because we had made it this far), and this made the Parkway a lot more appealing than the unknown perils of option one.

So, back on we went—gingerly. And sure enough, as we pulled up the ramp, there was the sign we'd missed the first time: "Merritt Parkway—Commercial Vehicles and Vehicles Over 8 Feet Prohibited."

The good news is that we made it back; the bad news is that we were sucked inexorably into the orbit of New York City. The traffic thickened, the roads narrowed, and the rain increased. And then came the Jersey Barriers, those concrete portable walls used to divide an active highway from a construction project. It is no fun to drive an RV in proximity to Jersey Barriers, especially at night on your First Time.

Next time you're behind a car, even a big SUV, notice how much road there is on either side of the tires: a couple feet, easy. Now check the side clearance on an RV: maybe six inches. This is why shoulders (the wider the better) are the RVers best friend—they provide a margin for error, a real and a psychological buffer. Jersey Barriers, on the other hand, are the antithesis of shoulders—not only do you not have any margin for error, but also there is something very hard right next to you just waiting to take the paint off your side and send you careening into the middle lane.

But we finally made it to the Tappen Zee. Never had I been so glad to be heading into New Jersey.

Finding an RV park under these circumstances was out of the question, but we had to stop somewhere. Although I had let Bob drive part of the afternoon, I decided that it really wasn't fair to put him in the position of being responsible for the Dutch Star, so I soon took back over—and was getting tired. (Having once driven the State Police Mobile Crime Lab, Bob did have some experience on me, but basically, neither of us knew diddly.)

Absent an RV park, the only remotely practical option was a thruway rest stop, although we quickly found that we wouldn't exactly blend in. We gingerly pulled in and around to the back of the restaurant—and there was an elephant's graveyard of eighteen-wheelers. There were dozens of them, lined up in hatchmark rows, most with their motors running—which gave the whole scene an erie background hum like the soundtrack of a Ridley Scott movie. And here we came with our cutsie green and gold paint job and gigantic windshield. I felt like a guy in a seersucker suit at a Harley rally.

I was sure a large man in a black t-shirt would come to the door with a tire iron and suggest we move on before something unspeakable happened to us in the back cabin of one of the trucks. You know, those dark places with names like "Work Room" and "Pleasure Palace" in script on the side.

But we were tired and out of options, so we crept into a slot between two huge rigs (as in eighteen-wheeler rigs, not RV rigs), locked the doors (which would have kept the guy with the tire iron out for about 26 seconds), and settled down to a distinctly uncomfortable night.

We did sleep, but neither of us ever fully dozed off. It wasn't because of uncomfortable beds or even the noise of the diesels on either side; it was more that uneasy feeling that keeps you from fully falling asleep in an airport or any other place you don't really belong.

Saturday was a new day—clear, bright, and the Garden State Parkway positively beckoned. I knew we were OK on the height because of our company for the night. If those guys could travel this road, so could we. (It wasn't the last time I used an eighteen-wheeler to reassure myself the road was safe height-wise—there were more than a few back roads, too, where I breathed a sigh of relief when I saw a big rig coming toward us. Wherever he had been, I reasoned, we could go.)

I did notice that when we approached the first toll booth, however, it was a tight squeeze. And like the guy who went by us in Connecticut blowing his horn, this was a warning. Which I again duly ignored.

The problem came when we were entering the Baltimore Harbor Tunnel. Another sign you've probably ignored all these years is the one that goes something like "No Hazardous Materials Allowed In Tunnel." Is propane (of which there was a big tank under our driver's seat) a "Hazardous Material" as used in this sign? Apparently in some places it is; in others it isn't. As we say in the law, this is not a settled question.

I wasn't sure about the rules for this particular tunnel, but I was very sure I didn't want to get off the highway to drive through a maze of downtown city streets on my second day of driving the bus.

So we decided to brazen it out and headed for the toll booth. I concentrated on charming the young lady collecting the tolls, hoping that my honest face and winning smile would keep her from noticing that I was driving a forty-foot RV that undoubtedly had enough propane on board to blow a nasty hole in her tunnel.

And it worked!

She smiled back, took my toll, and wished me a nice day. I hit the accelerator and positively basked in our good fortune—for about 1.8 seconds. At that point three things happened more or less simultaneously: Bob screamed something that sounded like "LOOK OUT" (very similar to his contribution of the previous night), there was a tremendous thump on the right side of the bus, and the passenger-side mirror disappeared.

I had just made the biggest RV rookie mistake of all—cutting it too close to some obstruction or another (in this case, a steel upright at the right side of the toll booth exit) and clipping off the side mirror. When we were shopping for the RV, one of the used units we looked at had all of fifty miles on it. It seems the new owner had knocked the mirror off while crossing a bridge on his way home with his wife in the passenger seat—and she refused to set foot in it again. It was a great deal.

So into the tunnel we went, with the pilot (me) slightly rattled and flying at least partially blind. Suddenly, everything went completely dark.

"I can't see, Bob, I can't see a thing!" I shouted, assuming that I was experiencing some kind of panic-induced blindness.

"Take off your sunglasses, Governor," Bob answered, trying (not very convincingly) to be respectful. They didn't treat me this way during my first term.

What came next was a real nightmare. We emerged from the tunnel into the blazing light (I was blinded again, but resourcefully solved the problem by replacing my sunglasses) and immediately realized what a disability it was to not have the side mirror. Quite simply, you have no idea what is going on behind or on the right side of the bus. To understand what this feels like, try closing your right eye while driving and don't look in either the right side-view or rearview mirrors. I guarantee you won't be able to do it for long, especially when you pass an on-ramp.

So we had to do something; the problem was, there was no place to do it. We were in a jungle of concrete—ramps in all directions, tight under-passes, no shoulders to speak of, and all the traffic on the East Coast flying by at 75 miles per hour. (Have you noticed how the effective speed limit—as opposed to the legal one—has crept up in the last few years? Sixty-five now seems to mean almost eighty.) Finally, we pulled onto a shoulder (of sorts) a little way outside the tunnel.

The good news was that the mirror was still there—hanging by the thread of the wires to the heater behind its shiny face. The bad news was that I had forgotten duct tape. This is a hard admission for anyone from Maine to make and I realize it will diminish my reputation among my former constituents, but there it is. We had nothing on board that even came close.

But I needed that mirror.

So we did the MacGyver thing—*MacGyver* was a TV show from the 80s, where the hero finds himself locked in a room with an atomic bomb and six hungry crocodiles, and all he has to work with is a paper clip, two laundry tickets, and a Swiss Army knife. Each episode, he ended up building a short-wave radio or celestial telescope or some other impossibly complex device and miraculously got out of that week's jam.

What we had was a plastic pen, a pocketknife (not even Swiss Army), an extension cord, and an assortment of screwdrivers and wrenches. After a great deal of stopping and starting (and worrying that we would be hit by a wayward truck blowing past), here's what we did:

1. Took the mirror apart and pulled out the broken piece—the vertical steel pin that connected the mirror to the brace still attached to the side of the bus.

2. Used the knife to cut off both ends of the extension cord and split it up the middle, producing two pieces of wire, each about six feet long.

3. Unscrewed (slightly) the base plate of the still-intact brace, opening up a little crack between it and the body of the bus.

4. Cut the pen to the right length and forced it into the hole in the brace where the broken steel pin had been, then forced the mirror down over the pen.

5. Used the wire to support the mirror, running the wire around the mirror and back to the side of the bus, securing it in the crack under the base plate (see step 3), then tightening the plate down, thus holding the wire in place.

It sure wasn't pretty (it looked like one side of the bus had run through a giant spider web), but it worked. We had to stop every now and then and climb out to adjust the mirror (which made me appreciate the electric mirror adjusters in the car), but at least it gave me some vision—and proved extremely useful later in the day when we kept hitting merges on I-95 that would have been impossible without some awareness of what was going on to starboard.

The rest of the trip that Saturday was uneventful, unless you count the truly harrowing passage just south of Washington, D.C., where I-95 and the infamous Washington Beltway intersect. We made it through all right, but it sure wasn't the kind of idyllic driving you see in the ads for RVing.

We entered Williamsburg late in the afternoon and settled into the American Heritage RV Park, the Dutch Star's home until all of us returned in January. To be honest, I was awfully relieved that this part of the journey was over.

Only later did I realize that the worst stretch of driving on the whole trip was already behind us.

TRANSITIONS

All of us face transitions from time to time—school to work (maybe the hardest one of all—what ever happened to that summer-long vacation?), job to job, home to apartment, single to married, married to single (alas), parent to grandparent—and every one involves emotional, financial, or psychological challenges. One of the hardest, however, is the transition many of us baby boomers currently face—from the peak of our career (supervisor, CEO, principal, full-time parent, or, heaven help you, governor) to…well…nothing. In other words, retirement.

Actually, "retirement" really isn't the right word these days. Most of the sixty-somethings I know don't go to the same office or put on a tie every day, but neither do they spend all their time in a rocking chair or on the golf course, either. Instead, they work a variety of jobs, some paying and some non-paying, at home and out of the house. I think we need a new term to describe these people, something like "post-careerer" or "full-time part-timer" or, the current favorite among many of my friends, "consultant."

Whatever you call it, leaving the power and perks (not to mention the money) of your real job for the amorphous whatever-comes-after ain't easy. It takes serious thought and planning—and hopefully the financial planning part started a long time before the real exit. It also takes a mental shifting of gears, a psychological confrontation with your new, somewhat diminished place in the universe. This realization has to happen, but it needn't happen all at once, and coping with it should not be your sole occupation. In other words, ease into the change, and keep busy while it rolls over you.

Such as by taking your family on a six-month road trip.

I wish I could say that our trip was part of a well-thought-out scheme, carefully calibrated to help me manage the transition from governor to private life—but I can't. Instead, it was a happy accident—it makes perfect sense as a transition strategy, in retrospect, but it wasn't a big part of the original decision.

Looking back on the experience, here's what I learned:

1. Have a life before the transition hits. In other words, maintain some balance. Tie flies, get to know your kids, read novels, travel—anything outside of work, so that what you're transitioning to isn't wholly new. "I'm going to take up golf as soon as I leave the job" won't cut it—what if you hate the game? Our practice trip to Arizona, for example, was important so we could be sure that the concept made sense; six months in a bus with four people could have been a disaster if the chemistry wasn't right.

2. Start your planning before you leave the job. This gives you something to look forward to and keeps you from getting maudlin about the good old days you haven't even left yet. This also makes it possible to…

3. Have something to do the very first day; moping around feeling useless for even a few days is a recipe for depression.

4. Whatever you do next should be engaging. Notice I didn't say *important* or *significant.* In my case, it involved shifting from worrying about what the Legislature would do to worrying about whether the next RV park would have a dump station. The key word here is "worrying"; in other words, something should occupy your mind so you don't dwell on the fact that nobody cares anymore about what you say.

5. Let go of the old job. I didn't read any Maine newspapers or obsessively stay in touch with my friends back home at any point during the trip. Second-guessing while at the same time being helpless is not a worthwhile use of your time. Worry about that dump station; now that's *important.*

6. While not mandatory, travel is a good idea. It literally takes you away from your accustomed surroundings and all your associations with the old job, which in turn makes it easier to move on emotionally as well as physically. "Changes in latitudes, changes in attitudes," as the Bard of our generation, Jimmy Buffett, has observed.

7. Take a chance; be a little crazy. This is your big opportunity to live a dream you may have harbored since childhood—join the circus, sail the seas, climb a mountain, or write a novel. Don't listen to that little man sitting on our shoulder whispering "you can't do that; what will people think?" You can and you should. A much better question than "why?" is "why not?"

And, of course, enjoy the trip!

2

First Leg
Racing Winter from Maine to Florida—and Losing

Maine to Virginia and into the RV

s I mentioned, it was Mary's brilliant idea to take the RV to Virginia in the fall so we wouldn't have to leave Maine in a January snowstorm in a forty-foot bus (with a guy driving who hadn't been behind the wheel of anything in eight years). So we left Brunswick, Maine, in Mary's fully packed Honda van headed for (I'm not making this up) Hoboken, New Jersey, home of my son Duncan and future daughter-in-law, Emily Dancyger.

This wonderful sign mysteriously appeared at the end of our driveway the morning we left. Whoever did it, thanks; it meant a lot.

This is one loaded van—I know, it needs a wash.

Why live in Hoboken? Not a bad view, for starters.

Molly and the cabs—since we didn't need one.

We realized that no matter what we did in the way of home schooling (in this case, it should be called "road schooling"), there would be plenty of education along the way. On our first day in New York, we took the PATH train under the Hudson and walked from 33rd Street and Sixth Avenue to the *Intrepid* Museum on the Hudson at 46th. After exploring the Second World War aircraft carrier and the *Growler,* one of the first Cold War nuclear missile submarines (which made the RV look spacious inside), we made our way back to Herald Square for a couple hours in Macy's, the World's Largest Store—it said so on the sign

The next couple days in New York included the Metropolitan Museum of Art (Ben liked the armor, Molly the Tiffany windows); lots of *walking* (the kids learned one of the basic facts about New York—there are lots of cabs around when you don't need them, but if you're tired and it starts to rain, they all disappear or flip on the "Off Duty" sign); dinner with friends in the

Village (that's Greenwich, not Wiscasset); poking around the lower East Side; bridal shopping; a wonderful performance of the *Pirates of Penzance* (Ben said that Gilbert and Sullivan were the Capitol Steps of a hundred years ago); walking to Times Square for several hours of arcading (OK, so it's not all education) at the ESPN Zone; and all sandwiched between various pieces of the NFL playoff games. (What happened to the Jets? What always happens to the Jets?)

On Monday, we headed south on the New Jersey Turnpike to visit friends from Maine, James and Meg Smith, who live right in the middle of the Naval Academy grounds in Annapolis. James is a Navy Captain who teaches at the Academy (Meg is a Commander in the Reserves) and we got to know them when he was in charge of one of the new ships built at Bath Iron Works, near our home in Maine. This was real education for the kids: a tour of the Academy, including a terrific film on what it's like to be a midshipman, the most incredible ship-model collection, the spectacular chapel, and several visits to the campus store. I had hoped Ben might become interested in the Naval Academy—and its free college education—but to no avail.

From Annapolis, across the Bay Bridge, and down the Delmarva Peninsula ("Why is it called Delmarva?" I asked, assuming the role of teacher—they figured out it meant Delaware, Maryland, Virginia), we made it to Williamsburg and the waiting RV. Despite sitting for two months, it started right up, and we moved to a site, hooked up (Ben was in charge), and we were in business. We spent the next couple days unpacking, working on systems (these things are complicated—water, heat, satellite,

After months of planning and anticipating, we woke up in the middle of a freak Virginia snowstorm.

generator, and every other electronic gadget you can imagine), and just getting settled. One morning, we visited Jamestown—the kids wanted to know why the Pilgrims got all the credit when Jamestown was settled fourteen years before Plymouth. "Better PR" was my answer.

Then, after months of planning and anticipating (including the fall trip), we woke up—you guessed it—in the middle of a freak Virginia snowstorm. The local news folks had their "StormCenter" hats on and reported live (I'm not making this up) from the top of a salt pile. I felt right at home. So, we visited with family (my mom and sister and brother-in-law), started home schooling (Ben got a 98 on his math test), listened to music (satellite radio is so cool), and now simply had to wait.

Once we got going, our first stop was Kittyhawk, North Carolina, where we visited our friends Drew and Lisa Wright, and their three sons, who are, naturally, the Wright Brothers.

Remember Mary's idea of driving the RV down from Maine in November to avoid New England in January? Well, the concept was right, but here we are on the day of our scheduled departure for North Carolina—snowed-in in Williamsburg. There was a "freak" snowstorm the day we arrived, and another (6 to 8 inches this time) a few days later. So much for "freak."

Ben and I are hooking up the car for the first time. Like everything else, it seemed complicated at first, but several repetitions made it feel routine. Once underway, you don't even notice that the car is following. Wide turns are a good idea, however. We saw a bumper sticker on one such car (a "toad" in RV talk) with the wonderful message, "Sorry to be so slow, but I'm pushing this big RV."

Williamsburg Through the Outer Banks

The salient fact about the trip so far is that it is *cold*. Every time we inch south, the Weather Channel tells us about a new record low in Atlanta or Orlando. One morning, the kids suggested we scrap the whole trip (37 degrees on the South Carolina border—there was ice on the ground) and head to Mexico. Ben's alternative suggestion was to return to Maine where "you can at least have fun in the cold." We headed from Williamsburg to and through North Carolina's Outer Banks—a beautiful place no matter the weather.

We had a quiet trip after finally escaping (so far) the snow in Tidewater, Virginia, on Saturday. My handy *Truckers' Digest* warned of a low overpass on I-64 sou████████████████ through Portsmouth to the North Ca██████████████████ we headed southeast to the Outer Banks, the spectacular barrier islands along the Atlantic coast. Our plan there was to visit our friends the Wrights and their three boys, who we knew from the summer in Maine. We made it down a very narrow road and parked in their absent neighbors' driveway (the Wrights' was too short), and we arrived at their house just in time for a wonderful sunset over the Sound.

On Sunday afternoon, we had an amazing experience—driving with the Wrights right on the beach, all the way north to the Virginia border. Along the way, we passed fishermen, walkers, lots of other drivers (pickups were the order of the day), and a bunch of what looked like volunteer firemen setting a gill net in the surf. There is no road here—the beach is the

Here I am, doing just what we had hoped to miss—de-icing the top of the slide-out, determined to get on the road, albeit a day late. (RV Tip of the Day: If snow is expected, close the slide-out.) Second Tip: hot water works well, but having the sun out sure helps.

only thoroughfare—and there were big houses being built along the dunes, with all the materials (and the occupants) getting there across the sand. Don't try this in Maine.

The most stunning thing about this area is the amazing number of what can only be called mansions—really big houses, five-plus bedrooms, three and four stories, row after row, on tiny lots, all straining for a view of the ocean. Unlike many other oceanfront areas, the Outer Banks is the land of the single-family house as opposed to condos and apartments. I drew two conclusions: 1) buy waterfront real estate, wherever, whenever, and however you can; and 2) this is a very wealthy country. We saw something like half a billion dollars worth of (mostly part-time) houses in only about an hour.

Of course, the highlight of the trip was the trip to Kill Devil Hills—the site of the first powered flight, on December 17, 1903. If you just let go and try to imagine the scene a little more than a hundred years ago, it's an awesome (in the truest sense of the word) experience.

The North Carolina coast rivals the Maine coast in at least one respect—lighthouses. Here is the Currituck Light, just north of Kitty Hawk. The Outer Banks seem to have at least one light about every twenty miles.

The monument was impressive and offered a commanding view of the surrounding island, but it was the simple stones indicating the take-off and landing points and a replica of the sixty-foot launch track that made the hair stand up on the back of my neck. The more you learn about this extraordinary milestone, the more you realize that the Wright brothers were more than mere tinkerers who stumbled upon a secret that had eluded man for all the ages past. They were authentic geniuses who used a combination of self-taught engineering (they discovered that the fundamental calculations of lift on a wing were wrong), American ingenuity, and plain hard work (they made more than 1,000 glides at Kitty Hawk over three years before trying it with a motor) to literally go where no man had gone before. In the case of the first flight, that was exactly 120 feet through the air.

Doin' (the) Charleston

If you're tired of seeing pictures of the RV in the snow, think how we felt. Yes, this is North Carolina, the southern part, no less. We're in Wilmington (home town of Sonny Jurgenson, Roman Gabriel, and Michael Jordan) and what this picture doesn't show is just how *cold* it was—about 15 degrees. What it also doesn't show is that furnace failed to light the night before and we had to limp through the night with two electric space heaters (the trick was to plug them into different circuits to keep from blowing the fuse) and a hundred-watt light bulb in the

On the right is Darrell Collins, for 25 years one of the park guides at the Wright Brothers' National Historic Site. But he is no ordinary guide—he is a historian, a born public speaker (I'll bet there's some southern country preacher in his genes), and a purveyor of dreams. It's pretty hard to hold the attention of a bunch of 10- and 12-year-olds during a history lecture, but he did it—with a combination of sheer knowledge (there seemed to be no question about the Wrights that he couldn't answer) and genuine passion.

Here is one of the many spectacular houses on the Battery, the small park at the end of the peninsula that constitutes downtown Charleston. If you turned ninety degrees to the right, you'd be looking out into the harbor toward Fort Sumter and the open sea.

plumbing compartment to keep the pipes from freezing. Naturally, being from Maine, we also knew to keep the faucets dripping.

Feeling pretty smug, I closed the biggest slide-out as soon as it started to snow, so no pictures of me de-icing this time.

The first RV shop we went to couldn't repair the furnace because they didn't have the part they had identified as the culprit. They located the part, but it was at Camping World in Myrtle Beach (about a hundred miles down the road, mercifully in the direction we were headed), and arranged for us to get the repair done there. So off we went, relieved to at least have a line on getting the heater fixed. The only problem was that when we got to Camping World, the damn furnace worked. And worked. And worked. Try as they might, they couldn't make it fail. The furnace fired up every time and the part passed the bench test with flying colors. It reminded me of taking a kid with a cough to the pediatrician—they'd hacked all night, but once you got them in the office, nothing. Well, that was our furnace.

What would you do? A replacement for a part that worked wasn't covered under the warranty; on the other hand, I knew *something* hadn't worked the previous two nights. So I bought some insurance and had them put the new part in anyway, assuming that if the old one had failed once, it might again, and I just didn't want to go through the light bulb in the plumbing thing again. Even though it wasn't covered under the warranty, it was still worth the peace of mind.

The next day, we began to explore Charleston. It was something of a milestone, since it was one of our original destinations when we first started planning the trip. And it's a beautiful place. The architecture reminded me of my hometown of Alexandria, Virginia, only more grand.

We did a ninety-minute guided tour with Marvin, whose business is called, naturally, "Doin' the Charleston" (yes, the dance was invented here in the 1920s). He has a great idea—in addition to driving by the various landmarks and describing their history, he has a TV and DVD player at the front of the bus so you can simultaneously see the interiors of buildings and pictures of the city's historic figures and events. It was like two tours for the price of one and gave us ideas about places we wanted to visit. Imagination is the key to entrepreneurial success, whether it's cars, computers, or trolly tours.

Charleston really is a charming city, even though I don't think we had the full experience because it was so cold. We missed the casual walks through antebellum neighborhoods and coffee in sidewalk cafes, but we still saw and learned a lot. Such as the fact that South Carolina was the first state to secede because its entire economy in the nineteenth century was dependent (they thought) on slavery.

We did do some touring, however—along the Battery and the seemingly endless side streets, down King Street from Planet Smoothie to the high-end shops near the old open-air market, and through the market itself with tables and booths of local crafts and Civil War t-shirts. To my amazement, I ran across a print of Maine's own Joshua Chamberlain leading the charge down the hill at Little Round Top.

One of our stops was the terrific Charleston museum, the oldest museum in the United States. It was very well done, with a lot of local history; I found

These two churches face each other across Charleston's main square. Notice how tall and narrow the towers are—never was the word steeple more accurate. It looks like the two congregations were competing to see who could get closer to heaven.

Remember education? On a trip like this, it takes place all the time and all over the place. For example, here's Mary and Molly at the Charleston Aquarium at a hands-on tank of various sea creatures. If it's possible to photograph the elusive "teachable moment," this is it.

Molly at a smaller tank with the tropical guys. I can never get over the colors.

Ever notice how you can tell it's your kid, even in silouette—here's Ben looking at the birds.

Speaking of downtown, how's this for a theater marquee? I don't want to know what you have to do to get an award in gastroenterology, but whatever it is, the lawyers are on it.

the images of slavery on the rice plantations especially moving, and appalling. Now, barely a hundred fifty years later, we are incredulous that such an institution could exist in our midst, and somewhat piously judge those benighted souls who maintained and fought for it. I devoutly hope that we are, in fact, more enlightened; but which of us would brave the censure of our peers, given a different context? The vote for secession at the South Carolina convention of December 1860 (the precipitating factor was Lincoln's election a month before), for example, was unanimous.

The Aquarium was cool; it had the usual big tanks with sharks, turtles, huge sea bass, and a supporting cast of thousands. (I've never understood how they get the sharks to swim around with all those other fish without eating them up. Are they on Weight Watchers or something?) A friend of mine refers to aquariums as "fish zoos," but this one went further. There was a mountain steam, complete with otters, a lot of hands-on tanks, and even some exotic birds.

OK, so it wasn't all education; after a couple of hours at the Aquarium, we went next door to see *The Lion King* at the IMAX. You haven't lived until you've seem Pumbaa and Timon on a screen five stories high.

On our final day in Charleston, Ben and I visited the aircraft carrier *Yorktown.* It's our third naval-vessel museum in as many weeks, plus the visit to Annapolis—this wasn't a conscious tilt toward the Navy, but it just seemed to happen. In the afternoon, we all went to Fort Sumter, where we met another terrific National Park guide, learned a lot, and ran into our first people from Maine (it had to happen sooner or later).

Savannah and Beaufort—Trolley Tours and Sprawl

Travel from Charleston to Savannah was pretty easy; I was gradually getting the feel of the RV. Just before we left Maine, I saw Representative Dick Maillot—my RV mentor over the course of the previous year. Dick's parting advice was "Always take your time, and remember, you're not driving a Corvette." He sure was right; every time I got into trouble, it was because of hurrying and not taking full account of the size of the vehicle.

We got to Savannah at about 2:30 in the afternoon (RV Tip: It's always better to arrive in the day-

This poster stands at the entrance to the Fort Sumter museum where you catch the boat out into the harbor. The flag in the background is a replica of the one that flew over the fort the morning of April 12, 1861 when the Confederate bombardment began. The remnants of the real one are in a case just below.

Here's what I looked like at work on a blog update. Notice the two-finger typing technique; it wouldn't do to be able to type faster than one thinks anyway. Once an update was complete, I sent it to the website via phone hook-ups at the RV parks. The phone line is most commonly found in the laundry room.

Here's Mary; ain't she great?

And here are John and Beth Hodgkins of Yarmouth, Maine. He is retired from the Maine DOT and we had met at the annual Blaine House maple tree tapping the spring before.

light) and went to the park we had picked from the RV bible, *Trailer Life's Camping Guide.* Only it wasn't so great. It was too close to the highway, the sites were scruffy, and it just wasn't very appealing. So we sacrificed the two nights rent we'd already paid and moved a half hour away to a beautiful Georgia state park. It was a much better site. Besides, my son James was coming over from Atlanta for a visit and we wanted to put our best RV foot forward.

Old Savannah is the most beautifully laid-out city in the United States. It has a straightforward grid design, but there are lovely little park-like squares every few blocks and wonderful trees (draped with Spanish moss) lining every street. The effect is incredibly serene, and it doesn't hurt that the squares are surrounded by graceful antebellum houses, some dating back to the mid-eighteenth century. Believe it or not, "antebellum" was one of the kids' vocabulary words on the first week of the trip; they've now heard it on every one of our tours.

Notice I said "Old Savannah"; just as was the case in Charleston and would be the case at Beaufort (pronounced Bew-fort), South Carolina, these stunning old downtowns are surrounded by some of the worst sprawl

I've seen anywhere. There's mile after mile of strip malls, traffic in all directions, franchise eateries (we even had dinner in a Red Lobster, where a boiled Maine lobster was $19.00—wish more of that made it to our fishermen), and billboards everywhere. Maybe it's just impossible to do quality urban design around our larger populations and the automobile, but the contrast of how we live today with these old towns is absolutely jarring and makes It all too obvious what we've lost.

One of the best ways to get to know something about a town In a short time is to take a local tour—a trolley reproduction (no tracks) seems to be the style these days—and then you can go back to the spots that seem interesting.

Speaking of tours, all these old Southern towns seem to have a lot of ghosts—each one offers a variety of ghost tours, both walking or riding (left). Ben wanted to go on one, but I passed. It didn't take much imagination (even in broad daylight) to see that those squares and Spanish moss would be pretty creepy at night.

No pictures of the sprawl, per se, (just look out your window), but I thought these signs near Savannah were funny. If you can't read the line under the Hooters sign, it says, "We are the people your parents warned you about."

After two days in Savannah, we drove back up the coast to Beaufort, South Carolina, another beautifully preserved town with incredible houses and a rich history intertwined with early Spanish settlers, island plantations, slavery, and the Civil War. It is also the home of one of America's greatest writers, Pat Conroy, who has immortalized the region in books such as *The Prince of Tides, The Water Is Wide,* and *The Great Santini.* I was surprised (and impressed) that our tour guide grew up with Conroy.

And I think this one should get some kind of award for getting straight to the point. Don't the prices look quaint?

I like the "Est. 1513" part.

I should note how we traveled when we went on those side trips—not in the RV. We towed Mary's car and our routine was to find a nice centrally located park, set up there for three or four days, and explore the area by car. In a sense, the whole trip was really a series of four-day visits strung together. Most people assumed we'd drive the RV every day, but it was much easier than that. Hitching or unhitching the car, by the way, only took about eight minutes.

Florida—Alligators, Henry Flagler, and the House of Wax

Yes, it was sunny the day we crossed into Florida, but it was still sweater weather. We were beginning to feel resigned to never quite escaping winter.

We took a combination of back roads and interstates to and through Florida—back roads are always better except for the fear of encountering a low underpass. As I mentioned, the RV was more than 12 feet high and suddenly those signs I'd ignored my whole life ("Low Bridge" or, worse yet, "Next Bridge 10'4"") took on a new and incredibly urgent meaning. (RV Tip: Welcome the sight of an oncoming eighteen-wheeler on a back road; whatever might come up on the road ahead, he was able to get under it.)

Our first stop in Florida was St. Augustine, one of the oldest European settlements in North America.

A fellow named Henry Flagler invented Florida as most of us know it—resorts, beaches, and thousands (now millions) of tourists, and it all started in St. Augustine. An associate of John D. Rockefeller, Flagler came to Florida in the 1880s and was disappointed with the accommodations.

So he began a thirty-plus year career of innovation and development, including grand hotels in St. Augustine, Palm Beach, and Miami, and a rail line from Jacksonville to Key West.

Flagler's St. Augustine hotel, the Ponce De Leon, is an unbelievable building; thankfully, when its time passed as a hotel, it became, appropriately, Flagler College, and has been beautifully preserved. Nowhere else in America do college students have their meals in a room surrounded by $20 million worth of Tiffany windows.

What looks like the hotel bell tower is actually a water tower; the Ponce De Leon was one of the first hotels in America with running water. Mr. Flagler also wanted another new-fangled convenience for his guests, electricity, so he hired the only electrician he knew at the time to come down and wire the hotel—a guy named Thomas A. Edison. This would be like having Bill Gates set up your computer network.

Here are Mary and Molly on the parapet of the Castillo San Marcos, the Spanish fort that stands guard over the bay at St. Augustine. This area has a bloody history (our ancestors seemed to fight most of the time) involving the Spanish, English, and French, as well as both sides in the Civil War.

CATHEDRAL
CLOSED
for
ORGAN
TRANSPLANT
Installation
of
3,000 pipe
Casavant organ
Reopens Saturday, Feb 15
5:00 p.m. Mass

No trip to St. Augustine would be complete without a visit to the Alligator Farm. I'm serious; this was a neat place. It was clean and well maintained, the people were nice, the animals were fascinating, and at feeding time we could hear the bones of the giant South American rats crunch like peanuts in the alligators' jaws. Now there's an evocative sentence, but not half as evocative as the real thing. Mary wasn't excited by it and went off to write postcards; Ben thought it was cool. A guy thing, I guess.

Another regular stop in St. Augustine is Potter's Wax Museum. Like everyone else my age, I remember being scared witless by *House of Wax* as a kid (remember the glasses?), and these places will always give me the creeps. They just look a little too, well, real.

The beaches really were beautiful. Notice, however, the complete absence of people, because it was so bloody cold. Mary and Ben salvaged the day by visiting an enormous outlet mall—is anything sold at full price anymore?

HISTORY

*"History doesn't always repeat itself,
but it usually rhymes."*
—Mark Twain

The Virginia Peninsula, Hampton Roads, Hatteras Inlet, Fort Fisher, Fort Sumter, Savannah, Atlanta, Mobile Bay, New Orleans, and dozens of other towns and country crossroads throughout the Deep South remind anyone passing that way of America's greatest tragedy—and its defining event—the Civil War. And our trip was no exception.

We entered Virginia from the east, across the Chesapeake Bay Bridge Tunnel, passing through Hampton Roads, where the first ironclads, the *Monitor* and the *Merrimac* (CSS *Virginia*) fought to a draw and changed the face of naval warfare forever. From then on for the next six weeks, we were never far from the echoes of this terrible conflict. To try to help us understand what we were seeing, we started watching segments of Ken Burns' epic miniseries, *The Civil War*. (If you haven't seen this lately, I urge you to buy it or rent it. In my view, it is the greatest documentary film ever made, enveloping the viewer in the sweep of the unfolding catastrophe in terms of both high-level strategy and its impact on individual men and women not much different from ourselves.)

In reflecting upon this segment of the trip in the context of the current state of American politics, I'm struck by the truth of Mark Twain's quote. If you go back to the speeches and rhetoric of the secessionists from the 1840s through the outbreak of the war (at Charleston's Fort Sumter, where we stood a month into our trip), you'll find passages eerily similar to what we're hearing today, complete with references to the Second and Tenth Amendments, enumerated powers, Jefferson's quote about watering the tree of liberty with the blood of patriots, interposition, nullification, the right of secession, and even the Boston Tea Party.

I'm old enough to have a sense of déjà vu about all this—no, not because I remember the Civil War; I'm not *that* old—because I came of age in the South of the 1950s, when exactly the same (and I mean *exactly the same)* arguments and impassioned rhetoric poured forth in response to the rising tide of the civil rights movement. Yes, the Civil War was about "states' rights," but not as an abstract principle, as some would argue. It was about a state's right to maintain slavery. Period. If you don't believe me, google "South Carolina Secession Declaration."

By the same token, everyone (on both sides of the civil rights debate) understood that all the state's rights-Tenth Amendment-tyranny of the 1950s federal government rhetoric wasn't being deployed in the service of some abstract principle of federalism; it was all about a state's right to maintain segregation. Period.

And now we're hearing it all again. But what's puzzling to me is that I can't figure out what's behind it this time. Federal deficits have been with us for fifty years, through Democratic and Republican administrations (it was Vice President Dick Cheney who famously quipped, "Reagan proved deficits don't matter"); in fact, the only balanced budgets in living memory were at the end of the Clinton administration. So it's hard to understand how deficits are suddenly cause for mass demonstrations. And is a mandate to buy health insurance or cap carbon emissions really enough to justify talk of secession and "Second Amendment remedies"?

No, something else is going on here whose outlines are not yet clear. It's not the same as our experience so long ago, but it's certainly beginning to rhyme.

NEWPORT NEWS   REBEL STEAMERS, JAMESTOWN & YORKTOWN.   CONGRESS.   SEWELL'S POINT.
CUMBERLAND   MINNESOTA

THE FIRST BATTLE BETWEEN IRON SHIPS OF WAR.

The "Monitor" 2 Guns and "Merrimac" 10 Guns
The Merrimac was crippled and the whole Rebel fleet driven off.

New Orleans to the Big Bend

Cousins, Acrobats, and Mom Takes the Wheel

The Big Easy

After leaving St. Augustine, we headed west along the Florida Panhandle in search of sun and a couple days with no tours or other educational activities. The kids had already announced that they never wanted to see another trolley and we were still 2,000 miles from San Francisco. After crossing into the Central time zone (a milestone of sorts), we stopped in Destin, renowned for its white powdery beaches and 350 days of sun a year.

And we hit three of the fifteen rainy days. Mom made it a learning experience by asking Ben what percentage of the fifteen rainy days we experienced (20% is the depressing answer). We did have a fun visit with friends Tom and Florence Schoener from Maine. Tom is retired from the Department of Inland Fisheries and Wildlife and Florence works part-time at the Blaine House. They are experienced RVers and invited us to visit them at their campsite nearby. Tom really helped my mood when he announced that they had been to the Panhandle five times and said, "this is the coldest day we've ever had."

Here's Ben doing one of his favorite things, driving the golf cart with Mary's cousin Bobette. We also had a visit with Bobette's daughter Heidi, her husband Igor, and their son Max.

I decided to grow a beard. I was hoping for a little more of the Sean Connery look, but it was probably closer to Willie Nelson.

Somewhere along this stretch, I decided to actually grow a beard; one friend in Maine tactfully suggested that I was starting to resemble Santa Claus. I was actually hoping for a little more of the Sean Connery look, but it was probably closer to Willie Nelson than anything else. Molly hated it.

From Destin, we drove west, through Pensacola, out of Florida, and through the little pieces of Alabama and Mississippi that front on the Gulf (which reminded me of the short slice of New Hampshire that divides Maine from Massachusetts). Everybody, even states, wants coastal real estate.

We settled north of New Orleans at the home of Mary's cousin, Bobette Szyller and her husband Avram. They very graciously allowed us to park the RV in their yard (I'm not sure they knew how big it was when they issued the invitation), and the kids loved the place.

Molly in Savannah, bravely letting the parrot remove a peanut from between her teeth.

One of the fun things in any city is the street entertainers, such as this young woman who stood stock still as the angel from the cover of *Midnight in the Garden of Good and Evil.* She only moved when you put money in the urn, which brought a stately bow.

Hack here really could play that trumpet; "Just a Closer Walk With Thee" brought tears to my eyes. And the beignets at Cafe Du Monde (where this picture was taken) really were delicious.

After a few spins in the golf cart, Ben reminded me that he would be able to get his learner's permit in just over two years and I kept trying to convince him that we raised the driving age to 18 just before I left office. He didn't buy it.

And then we went onto New Orleans and the French Quarter. Yes, the architecture was charming, but the scene had become so entirely touristy, it seemed to have lost much of its sense of authenticity. This is something we'd noticed before—places with some natural attraction, such as architecture, the seacoast, ambiance of some kind, are more or less ruined by the influx of people (like us) who want to experience them. It's as if the whole country (the interesting places, anyway) are becoming parodies of themselves, a kind of Disneyland writ large. As a friend in Maine once said about Bar Harbor: "We're loving it to death."

And how long have acrobats been performing on city sidewalks? These four recruited Ben to play a part in their finale, where one of the guys jumps over the whole crew, including "volunteers" from the audience. "Take my sister instead," were his last words before being carried bodily into the middle of the act.

Like I said, the tour was a little long; here's Mary about halfway through. We should have gone to the IMAX.

We did do a bus tour of the entire city; it was too long, but we learned some neat stuff. Did you know that New Orleans' nickname, The Big Easy, was possibly a reference by musicians in the early twentieth century to the relative ease of finding work there? It also may have originated in the Prohibition era, when the city was considered one big speakeasy due to the government's inability to control alcohol sales. Or that this term was bestowed by Ronald Reagan? Another fact we now all know is that the whole city is eight feet below sea level. That's why the graves are above ground—and why it was such a disaster when the levees broke during Hurricane Katrina.

I called my mother back in Williamsburg the day we got to town and told her where we were. She remembered coming to New Orleans with her dad for a railway agents' convention in 1923. That's more than ninety years ago, folks. And the thing she remembered most vividly? The above-ground cemeteries.

Anybody remember the film *Easy Rider*?

And finally, here are some shots of the French Quarter at night. We had a great meal at Galatoire's, but the rest of Bourbon Street was pretty rough. Colorful, but leave the kids at home for this part.

And I couldn't resist this one.

Tabasco, Zydeco, and Catfish Heaven

The French first came to North America in 1604, landing on a small island in the mouth of the St. Croix River near the present-day city of Calais, Maine. That was three years before Jamestown and seventeen before the *Mayflower*. For the next 150 years, French Catholic settlers lived in eastern Canada—they called it Acadia—in uneasy proximity to their British neighbors.

Then, in 1754, for reasons still somewhat obscure, the British literally drove them from their homes and lands in a kind of Anglo-Saxon pogrom, and a French diaspora began. Some Acadians moved west into French-

The making of Tabasco. The mash is aged in wooden barrels for up to three years, then it is mixed with vinegar and a little salt to make the magic sauce.

Here's Ben counting some of the stored barrels.

Sorry about the picture quality—this was taken through the RV's front window into the sun, but it still gives you a flavor of the local architecture. Mary loved it, as well as the local cuisine—so help me, she ate nine pounds of crawfish while we were in Louisiana. These little towns have drive-up crawfish shacks, just like lobster shacks in Maine.

And here's Molly checking out the barrels. Remember now, this product is literally used by the drop, so that's a lot of Tabasco you're looking at.

A real treat—breakfast at the Café Des Amis in Breaux Bridge on Saturday morning. The place was mobbed, the food was great, and the Zydeco music was fantastic.

Mom and Molly on the tiny dance floor; anybody who can sit still in the presence of good Zydeco is seriously lacking the fun gene.

speaking Canada, but many came to the U.S., principally to two widely separate places—northern Maine and southwestern Louisiana. Because both of these areas were geographically isolated, and because the Acadian people chose to keep substantially to themselves (and why wouldn't they, after what they'd been through?), their French language and culture remained largely intact until well after World War II.

Their descendents are the wonderful Acadians of the St. John Valley in Maine and the Cajuns (say Acadian five times fast) of Louisiana—and it's the latter we visited next.

We drove east on Interstate 10 from New Orleans about three hours to the little city of Breaux Bridge, then south to the even smaller city of St. Martinville, where we found our RV park, Catfish Heaven—which has to be the only combination RV park and catfish farm in the country.

The next morning we headed farther south—to the margin of the Gulf of Mexico—for what turned out to be one of the real highlights of the trip so far, a visit to Avery Island, the home of world-famous Tabasco Sauce. A friend of ours in Maine is associated with the McIlhenny Company, the owners of Tabasco, and she arranged a tour of the plant and the island.

The history of Tabasco is a classic American story: a New Orleans banker lost everything after the Civil War, returned to his wife's family land on the Louisiana coast, and experimented with sauces made from peppers grown on the property. His friends and neighbors liked the sauce and encouraged him to make some for them. Now, 135 years later, the sauce is sold in 104 countries and is the definitive hot sauce practically everywhere.

After the mash is mixed with vinegar, it's ready to bottle; here's a piece of the production line. The batch going through the morning we were there was bound for Singapore.

Molly in another teachable moment. The people at the plant were great. They didn't know us from Adam, but were friendly and obviously proud to be associated with the company. I've learned that one way to judge the culture (and likely success) of any company is by the loyalty of the workers.

And finally, after the plant tour, we took a boat ride around Avery Island. Here, Molly is driving the boat with the help of our wonderful tour guide, Dave Landry. We kept meeting people with names like Landry, Thibidoux, and Broussard; it felt just like home.

This is Hamilton Polk. He's a modern-day cooper who refurbishes and maintains the barrels (which can last up to 75 years) using a combination of modern technology and twenty-plus years of experience to produce small works of art. Ben said he wanted to come back and work for Ham. A boy could do a lot worse.

I always make it a point to kiss my wife after returning from an ocean voyage. So what if this one only lasted an hour?

Here's Molly putting the finishing touches on the ladyfingers—and paying close attention to the scrambled eggs.

If I put my left foot in where it's supposed to be, I kept hitting the brake. It only took me about ten laps to figure that out; I thought his car was just naturally faster.

The next morning was Valentine's Day and Molly had planned a major breakfast-in-bed production for Ben and me. Mom helped, but Molly had it all worked out—down to ladyfingers with strawberries and plenty of bacon, Ben's favorite.

The next day we did some home schooling, then went to Lafayette for some non-educational fun. We found the local equivalent of Joker's in Portland—arcade games, go-carts, pool, and Mary's new favorite, air hockey. Ricky Craven is safe from me; I did manage to pass Ben once, but my advantage was short-lived; he slipped by two turns later and I was toast.

Texas I—River Walk, the Alamo, and KOA

I always knew Texas was big, but it never really sunk in until we crossed the Louisiana line and the first sign we saw said "El Paso 898 miles." Wow, to an Easterner, that's a long way.

Our goal was San Antonio, but one jump from Breaux Bridge was too much, so we stopped Sunday night in Houston. Since it was to be only one night, Mary had the brilliant idea (she has lots of them) of foregoing the backing in and hooking up stuff and just stay in a motel. We only had two criteria: easy off and easy on the highway and an indoor heated pool. (Most of the RV parks we'd stayed at advertised heated pools, but none of them actually had them). So it was the West Houston Holiday Inn and a night of room service, movies on demand, and unlimited hot water.

The next day, we got to San Antonio, a neat city whose special character flows (couldn't resist) from the river that meanders through its heart. It's a perfect example of how something the planner-types call "an amenity" (and hard-nosed but short-sighted businesspeople sometimes call a frill) can have enormous economic, social, and cultural consequences. Texas as a whole takes in about $6 billion a year on tourism; San Antonio alone represents $4 billion of that total. And the River Walk, along with the Alamo, is what makes it happen.

The River Walk—it took ten years for the Ladies Conservation Council to persuade the all-male city council this was a good idea. The boys wanted to cover the whole thing over like a drainage ditch. Later came HemisFair in 1968, and the city came to life—around the River Walk.

The historical center of San Antonio (and all of Texas) is, of course, the Alamo— where a group of Americans from all over the country crossed the line Colonel Travis drew in the sand and died for independence from Mexico. They lost the battle, but the thirteen days they delayed Santa Anna's march gave Sam Houston enough time to build a sufficient force to finish the job a few weeks later.

The building wasn't all that impressive (smaller than I expected), and is set right in the middle of the city, but it conveys a very powerful message. There was a short movie at the nearby IMAX (is having an IMAX a sign of having arrived as a tourist destination?) on the battle that provided some background on what Travis, Crockett (yes, Davy—Molly insisted on a coonskin cap), Jim Bowie, and the few score of others accomplished.

The latest thing in urban landscapes is painted fiberglass animals. As you can see, in San Antonio it's cows. In Maine we've had bears in Belfast and lobsters in Rockland. No flies on us.

Visiting the Alamo was a very moving experience; it felt to me like a European cathedral. I was particularly affected by the list of the men who died there for an idea. The atmosphere is almost religious (the building was, after all, a Spanish mission); men took their hats off inside and voices were muted. It's a true shrine of the American experience.

We stayed at a KOA RV park in San Antonio (where the heated pool was even heated). KOA is the Holiday Inn of camping—no surprises, and consistent

It's hard to know where to start with the pictures, but as we headed into Texas, here's the view from the RV's bathroom window—what a way to start the day.

The road west; does this give you some idea why we're doing this?

I never knew what the term "azure blue" meant until I saw this.

Here are Ben and Molly tooling around the KOA kamp on the pedal rods rented at the kamp store. (Sorry, it's got me.)

We saw this rainbow just west of Del Rio, on the Mexican border, after a terrific storm.

quality. If only they didn't get so carried away by the "K" thing: stuff like "the Kampers Konnection," "kleen sweep," and "kabins and tents." K'mon.

From San Antonio, we left the big highway, and the countryside was more interesting and we just felt closer to it. There's something about interstates that seems to homogenize the views, as if the engineers built not only the road itself, but the adjoining half mile on each side. Yeah, on the side roads you have to slow down for the little towns, but in west Texas that was not a big problem. Besides, we would have missed this sign: "Go ahead and blink! Knippa is bigger than you think!" And it was—barely.

Texas II—Big Bend Country—Warm and Wonderful

We went to Big Bend National Park almost as an afterthought—driven mostly by the lousy weather everywhere else. What a lucky break—this

Our campsite (is it appropriate to call it camping when you bring along satellite TV, two cell phones, and dual air conditioners?) was about two hundred feet from the Rio Grande and thus the Mexican border. Those hills you see are in Mexico.

This is our first sunset in Big Bend National Park—after lots of towns and cities, our first off-the-beaten-track experience.

Another view on the way into Big Bend.

And how's this for one of your run-of-the-mill desert sunsets?

Here's Molly with new friends for life, Kate and Grace.

place is one of the gems of the country—unspoiled, varied, and inexpressibly beautiful. In this sense, it's sort of like the Grand Canyon—no photograph or description can do it justice. If you're ever thinking about a cross-country trip, put Big Bend on the list; its a bit out of the way, but well worth the detour.

We got to Big Bend via U.S. Route 90, which runs south of Interstate 10 out of San Antonio; essentially the same route as the interstate, but one tenth the traffic and much more interesting. We originally had visions of taking this trip entirely on "blue highways" and avoiding the interstates altogether, but that was before we fully understood the implications of driving a twelve-foot-high vehicle that can't be backed up (like at an unexpected low bridge) without unhooking the car, tying up traffic for half an hour, and generally being thoroughly embarrassed. The solution was a wonderful book called the *Professional Drivers' RoadAtlas,* which shows truck routes (interstates and others) in every state. This allowed us to depart the interstates with some degree of confidence. And as I mentioned earlier, there's nothing like the relief of meeting an eighteen-wheeler headed in your direction on an off-the-beaten-track road; you know you can go wherever he's been.

One of the great things that happened in Big Bend was that we met up with another family doing the same thing we were. Beth and Chris Powers had left New Jersey with their four kids about the same time we left Maine.

Ben and Molly at a nearby hot springs; behind Ben is the Rio Grande—about 55 degrees, while the water they're standing in is about 110 degrees. The hot water comes up from a hole at the side of the river—and sure felt good after a hike.

Mary and Molly on a "walk"; again, if you're wondering why we're doing this, this shot should supply a big part of the answer.

The gang in the midst of a climb (the mountain was about 6,000 feet, but we started at least half way up). Ben can't fully conceal the beginnings of a smile.

I make fun of Mary sometimes for picking up every brochure, guidebook, and map of wherever we're going to visit next, but over and over, it pays off. In this case, as we were walking in (we learned to call it "walking" as the kids wouldn't go on a "hike"), she produced a pamphlet on wild animal tracks in the Big Bend country—education of the best sort.

Molly with the tracks book at the edge of the Rio Grande—"Now, is it a mink or an otter?" My only contribution was to make bad otter jokes. You otter think up a couple yourself.

On the way back, we stopped at the world's most scenic pay phone. Here's Mary talking to her mom from Castolon.

The kids immediately bonded and the parents loved having someone else to swap home-schooling stories with ("you mean yours won't do cursive practice, either?").

Texas III—Canyons, Telescopes, and Mom Takes the Wheel

On our last day at Big Bend, we went to one of the park's most spectacular spots, Santa Elena Canyon. I'd been complaining about the weather since we left Virginia in that snowstorm in late January; in many ways, we were about a month early all along the route. The upside of this, however, was that we had many places, such as the Santa Elena Canyon, to ourselves. On this beautiful day, for example, we saw a total of six other people. It probably makes wearing a sweater every now and then worth it.

OK, now a little confession. We had this satellite TV, see? Only it wasn't really working very well. There were two problems—just when we got it all lined up to watch CNN or the Disney Channel, it switched by itself to the pay-per-view channel and we had to switch it back. As if that wasn't annoying enough, after we switched back to the original channel, the dish

We all went for a raft trip down the Rio Grande. Mom and the kids resisted, but I insisted. I was right (see why it's an advantage to be the guy who writes the history?). It was spectacular.

Ben got a chance to show off his paddling skills, while the guides told us tales of cowboys, Mexican wars, flash floods, and incredibly hot summers. Visit Big Bend in the winter or spring; 110 degrees isn't unusual in July and August.

Mary liked the whole deal so much, when we stopped for lunch she just couldn't hold it in. That's a happy lady.

After the raft trip, which took all day, we had dinner at The Boathouse in Terlingua; what a setting! You can see the sunset through the open-air bar where I met a guy from (you won't believe this) Skowhegan, Maine!

Headed out of Santa Elena. I have to pinch myself, it's so beautiful.

Beard watch: how could a guy so young have such a white beard? Was it the governorship or the kids? We're moving slowly from Willie Nelson to Kenny Rogers. But please, not Santa Claus.

would start to move and we'd lose the signal and have to start all over. It was pretty frustrating, especially after two months.

Well, it got so bad, I was finally driven to read the directions. Guess what? Switching to Channel 200 (which happens to be the pay-per-view schedule) was part of the dish's signal-fixing routine and we were supposed to leave it there for thirty seconds, then everything would be set. So when we immediately switched back (without waiting the requisite thirty seconds), we confused the dish into thinking it had the wrong signal, so it went looking for another satellite.

Mary thought this was hilarious; so maybe I'll read the directions next time, but I'll still never ask for directions, and don't even talk to me about the remote.

Our stay in Big Bend pointed out one of the best things about the trip which was that we didn't have much of an itinerary—no deadlines and no particular destinations. This meant that we could follow the weather or tips from fellow RVers—who tend to be a gregarious bunch with lots of advice. That's how we got to Fort Davis, Texas ("cool observatory"), a great stop we

Look who's driving the big kahuna! Mary took the wheel from Big Bend up to Alpine. There would be more miles at the helm in her future.

Jim and Judy Spradley showed me how a real cowboy hat is made, and we became friends at the same time. Did you know that a good hat is made of beaver fur? Or that when it's finished, it's literally sanded to make it smooth?

One last view of Big Bend country, coming out of Santa Elena Canyon. Is it any wonder we fell in love with this extraordinary place?

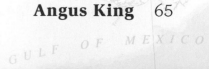

The officers' quarters on the parade ground at Fort Davis. The fort was set up to protect travelers from Apache raiding parties in the nineteenth century and was a fascinating window into this period of our history.

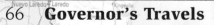

The business end of the 107-inch reflector at the McDonald Observatory, once one of the world's largest and still in everyday use. Just about my favorite toy as a kid was a four-inch reflector I got one Christmas.

most certainly would have missed had we tried to set up our stops months in advance. And I wouldn't have gotten to order a custom-made cowboy hat at the Limpia Creek Hat Company, located on the main drag (sure enough, Mary read about it in a brochure on the region).

One of the most interesting things about the old fort in town was that it was home to a regiment of African-American cavalrymen after the Civil War—the famous Buffalo Soldiers. Remember the great Bob Marley song? There is a certain irony, I think, in black soldiers fighting Native Americans on behalf of white politicians.

Our final day in Texas was spent up the road from Fort Davis at the wonderful McDonald Observatory—a world-class facility perched in the Davis Mountains about 75 miles south of the New Mexico border. We went to a nighttime "star party," where everyone sat outside under one of the most beautiful night skies I had ever seen (that's why they built the observatory there) to get a quick astronomy course before taking turns looking through a variety of telescopes. Even if you've seen a million pictures, there was still something neat about seeing the rings of Saturn "live."

NO PLAN

Itinerary? We Don't Need No Stinkin' Itinerary

Probably the best plan we had for the trip was not having a plan.

When we left Brunswick, we had a vague idea of circumnavigating the country and ending up back home in mid-June so the kids could rejoin their classes for the last week of school, but that was about it. And not having a specific plan or itinerary turned out to be the perfect way to approach the trip, for a variety of reasons.

The first is that most of us don't realize the stress we put ourselves under just in the way our lives are scheduled. Jonathan Swift once wrote a piece of satire about people who walked around with little dictators on their arms who told them what to do and when to do it—isn't that a great description of the calendar in your iPhone? Most of us are slaves to a schedule —when to get up, go to work, take a coffee break, attend meetings, eat lunch, get a haircut, pick up the kids at soccer; even our social life is duly set in little two-hour calendar entries. And each one involves a deadline.

The result is a constant low-level pressure about what's coming up and whether we'll be on time for the next appointment. (Have you ever thought about the very phrase "on time?" Just the term carries a hint of tension.) Of course, as governor, I was scheduled within an inch of my life. Every morning I got up and the fax machine in the kitchen (a bad sign in itself) spat out my day's schedule in twenty-minute increments—as many as a dozen meetings, interspersed with bill signings, office tours with unexpected fourth-graders, and an emergency session on some crisis that had arisen since the schedule was prepared the afternoon before.

Coming from that—which differs only in degree but not in kind from the way all our lives are organized—having a day, actually about 180 days, with no schedule, no deadlines, no time pressure, was amazing. I had no idea the amount of strain I had been under until it went away. And I think most people would have the same reaction.

The other reason our "no-plan plan" turned out to be so important was that we would have missed so many great places and experiences along the way had everything been scheduled in advance. Probably the best example was Big Bend National Park.

We had vaguely heard of Big Bend before we left, but had also heard that it was probably too far out of the way for a visit, so we put it on the mental back burner. But when we were about to leave San Antonio, I looked at the weather map and saw that it was in the 40s and raining in New Mexico—our original next destination—and about everywhere else within striking distance. Everywhere, that is, except for a little tip of south-west Texas on the Rio Grande, where it was clear and 70 degrees —and right in the middle was Big Bend National Park.

So, having no deadlines in New Mexico, we headed south instead of north and discovered one of the most beautiful and interesting places in America. With a proper itinerary, we would have missed Big Bend—not to mention Mesa Verde, the Port Townsend Rhododendron Festival, and the fabulous Corn Palace in Mitchell, South Dakota.

So flexibility and spontaneity are the bywords—follow the weather, tips from fellow RVers, notes in local guidebooks, or your nose—to see more, have more fun, and (this is important) relax along the way.

New Mexico & Arizona
Under, Over, and Out of this World

4

One of our first stops in New Mexico just had to be Carlsbad Caverns. They're not the deepest or the longest caves in the world, but they have to be up there with the most beautiful and awe-inspiring. Pictures can't do justice to the unearthly atmosphere and our constant sense of surprise as we turned corners and found ever more fantastic shapes and textures. This was another stop where our being ahead of the season paid off. We went late in the day (2:00 pm is the latest they will let you walk in—and walking in is definitely the way to go) and we had the whole expanse of cavern virtually to ourselves.

The cave entrance was known from prehistoric times, but apparently wasn't entered until the nine-teenth century when sixteen year-old Jim White decided to see what was down in that forbidding hole. He was a brave kid; we got pretty nervous descending out of the sunlight even knowing it was a national park.

The other Cavern Tip is to spring for the three bucks and take the self-guided audio tour. There were numbered signs along the trail and the little "wand" whispered information about what we saw. The kids really got into this and admonished me when I skipped a lesson. (Lesson one—which I certainly didn't know—was that what is now the cavern was at one time a gigantic coral reef on the edge of an inland sea.)

The other thing I finally learned is the difference between stalactites and stalagmites. Stalactites hang down, so they have to hold on "tight" to the ceiling, while stalagmites stand up from the floor "mighty" and tall. Don't laugh—I bet you didn't know either.

I couldn't resist this one—millions of years of seeping water and imperceptible erosion to form a men's room 750 feet beneath the surface of the earth.

Just your run-of-the-mill roadside view as we entered New Mexico. One of the best things about the RV is the enormous windshield, which makes driving like sitting in the front row of an IMAX travel movie.

So we went to the International UFO Museum in Roswell. So what?

Before leaving Carlsbad, a word is in order about our national parks. They're great—well maintained, impressive (each in its own way), and, most particularly, staffed by courteous, pleasant, and dedicated people. From Kitty Hawk to Fort Sumter to Big Bend to Carlsbad, we found really nice people who were passionate about "their" place and who made us feel welcomed and valued as guests. People are always complaining about taxes, but whatever goes to these magnificent places is money well spent. We still don't need one in northern Maine, though.

The town of Roswell, New Mexico, will forever be associated with aliens and "Area 51." And so we had to check out the International UFO Museum, which turned out to be pretty cool. In 1947, there was a crash in the desert about forty miles from Roswell and the reports from the scene described an alien spacecraft with complete bodies (four feet tall, no hair, large oval eyes). A local cowboy who was in the back of his pickup with a lady friend (no details on that) saw it and was the first on the scene. Then the Air Force arrived (conveniently, there was a U.S. Air Force base right in Roswell), sealed off the area, and belatedly issued a statement that it was simply an errant weather balloon. Sort of an early version of "nothing to see here, just move along."

The rest is history, and some pretty unclear history at that. The museum is a non-profit entity (admission is, surprisingly, free) and tries hard to stay neutral. It's full of affidavits, newspaper and radio accounts of the time, and bits and pieces of "evidence" of what happened that night more than sixty years ago. The argument now is more about whether there was an official cover-up than about what actually happened. Sound familiar?

One of the most interesting displays was a huge world map with colored lights indicating UFO sightings around the world. What jumped out at me was that the vast majority of the "encounters" are in the U.S. (Remember *Close Encounters of the Third Kind?* We were headed to Devil's Tower!) Either the aliens really like us or we're the most suggestible people on earth. Guess which gets my vote.

How many versions of this shot are in photo albums around the U.S.?

And here are Molly and her friends Kate and Grace Powers, with an exclusively Rosewell coke machine.

Roswell's other museum is a wonderful combo—an art museum joined to an extensive exhibit on the life of rocketry pioneer Robert Goddard, who did most of his life's work in New Mexico. Both Mary and I were struck by this painting of N.C. Wyeth by his daughter Henriette, who lived and painted in the Roswell area.

Sure looks like Mannana Island in Maine in the background to me.

After the caverns and the UFOs, we drove west on one of the most interesting roads we'd hit so far—New Mexico Route 82 from Artesia, across the desert, up into the mountains, and down again to Alamogordo. And we saw our first snow since North Carolina. The road rose gradually over about eighty miles, then entered a beautiful series of mountain valleys that reminded us of Vermont or western Maine. Small farms gave way to summer houses (it's 70 degrees up there when it's 110 in the valley below) and ski condos. And then, around a bend came an amazing sight—an enormous desert valley with a huge patch of snow in the distance. Snow? In the desert? Well, the shot on the left is what we saw—what would you think?

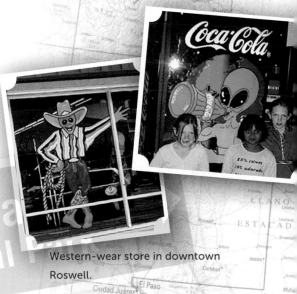

Western-wear store in downtown Roswell.

White Sands!

Ben flies from the top of the dune, and Molly was next—

Then Ben decided to try a makeshift snowboard, while Molly tried out her saucer and made a sand angel. A little slower than on snow, but it still worked.

Don't try this at home; it took us two days to get the sand out of ears, hair, and pockets.

It's white, all right, but it ain't snow. It's sand, made of gypsum with the consistency of talcum powder—the famous White Sands Missile Range and National Monument. What a sight, and a fun place to play, as you can see.

Arizona I—The Chiricahuas, Bisbee, and the Fabulous Shady Dell

Our strategy was still to stay south, close to the warm weather, so we temporarily skipped Albuquerque and Santa Fe and (again) headed west into southeastern Arizona, land of the Apaches, ghost towns, and Wyatt Earp.

Our first stop was the little town of Willcox, the hometown of Rex Allen, a cowboy movie star of the 1930s and 40s. Later, he narrated dozens of the Disney nature movies; you'd recognize his voice instantly (if you're over forty, that is).

But the real reason for stopping over in Willcox was that it is near the Chiricahua National Monument, a spectacular collection of unique rock formations created after a huge (1,000 times the power of Mt. St. Helens) volcanic eruption 27 million years ago. We drove the RV down from Willcox, parked in the visitors' center, ate a picnic lunch, and spent the rest of the day exploring this amazing place. I learned that, by and large, the digital camera doesn't do justice to places like this, but here's an idea of what it was like. The Apaches called it "Land of Standing Rocks," and they were right.

That evening, we drove south through a beautiful desert valley toward the Mexican border and the town of Bisbee,

The Shady Dell RV Park in Bisbee, Arizona. The coolest place we'd stayed so far. For two nights, we traded in the Dutch Star for a vintage Airstream and re-entered the fifties.

Wilcox, Arizona. Isn't this a classic western Main Street? The rail line is just across the park; there's no more romantic sound than a train whistle in the night.

One of the things that struck me over and over on this trip was how hard our predecessors had to work to build this country . . . it's easy to forget, but we stand on very broad shoulders.

Literally happy campers at the top of Sugerloaf Mountain near Chiricahuas. Ben's mountain-climbing style is to get to the top as fast as possible, turn around, and bolt down. He doesn't hang around for us to catch up and waste time on stuff like pictures.

which we'd learned about in another one of Mary's guidebooks, *Arizona, Off the Beaten Path.* Once the copper-mining capital of the world, Bisbee is now a tourist town with a funky artsy-historical-scenic charm. And the crown jewel of Bisbee, at least for us, was the Shady Dell RV Park. Driving in was like returning to the fifties—vintage RVs, Dot's Diner, and an old-fashioned friendly atmosphere. So we parked the Dutch Star and spent a couple nights in another era.

Remember the spoof record "The Flying Saucer," where they used cuts from popular records to tell the silly story? They had it. Unbelievable.

This is the inside of a 1952 Crown—twelve feet long and perfect for two. The radios are reproductions that disguise a tape player; the tapes supplied include Fats Domino, and Elvis.

Here are some of the units at Shady Dell—all for rent and all furnished in authentic 1950s accoutrements, right down to paint-by-numbers pictures on the walls, 78 RPM record players, and 1954 high-school yearbooks. It was fantastic and the whole thing just swallowed us up in a warm soup of nostalgia.

Notice the pink china and shiny ceiling; peeking out of the magazine rack is a 1955 copy of *Life*. Was life really simpler then, or is it just the lens of nostalgia? Will our grandchildren look back on "The Turn of the Century" (i.e., now) as a simpler and somewhat bucolic time? Heaven help them if they do.

And here's Dot's; the waitresses wore polka-dotted dresses, beehive hairdos, hankies pinned to their dresses, and had seams in their stockings.

Remember these? Ben had never seen one and insisted on calling the records "CDs"; he couldn't believe the mechanism that dropped the next record.

Downtown Bisbee, looking up at the Copper Queen Hotel, where we had a really excellent dinner our first night in town. Will Ben pass Mom in height before we return to Maine? He's about a half inch short; my money's on him.

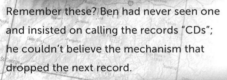

This is a corner of downtown Bisbee; the town is built on a series of steep hills and more than (literally) 3,000 miles of copper-mine tunnels. Dead when the mine closed down (2,100 people were laid off in one day in 1976), the town has come back to life as a haven for artists, artisans, restaurateurs, and, of course, tourists.

And here's the Dutch Star with its spiritual ancestor—a minor league baseball team bus. If you're headed to Arizona, forget Phoenix; check out the Shady Dell.

OK, so 50s music wasn't perfect, but have you heard what fourteen-year-olds are listening to these days?

One of the things that struck me over and over on the trip was how hard our predecessors had to work to build this country: Miners who worked twelve-hour shifts for $3.50 a day, slaves who grew rice in the tropical heat of South Carolina, Lewis and Clark's incredible three-year journey across the continent (the first thousand miles was all upstream), the young men and women of the CCC who built most of the infrastructure of our national parks, the soldiers on both sides of the Civil War—all endured physical challenges and discomforts we can only imagine. It's easy to forget, but we stand on very broad shoulders.

What's with this? All over town, some wag had painted out the "PAR" of "Parking." What a way to make a guy feel welcome; I'm glad nobody thought of this when I was in politics in Maine.

And I really got a little paranoid when I saw this sign; but if you look closely, there's an "i" in the name of the street. Whew.

The gang about to tour the Copper Queen Mine—a fun trip complete with slicker, head lamp, and a ride into the mine on a narrow-gauge train.

Here's a snowman (he's looking through binoculars into the Grand Canyon) Ben made the day we left the canyon. He then made another snowman of someone jumping over the edge. Imaginative child.

Those two specks you see in the left center are Ben and Mary; the drop at the turn is at least a thousand feet.

And of course, never go hiking without your walking stick. Here's Molly with hers—Mom got it in Big Bend National Park.

Arizona II–The Grand Canyon, Junior Rangers, and Travel Below the Rim

No picture, movie, written description, or painting can prepare you for the Grand Canyon. In its sheer size, complexity, variety, and overwhelming spirit, it is truly one of the earth's most extraordinary places. We spent three days in, along, and around it, and came away with a sense of wonder along with plans for our next visit. But first, a word about getting there.

The important fact to know is that Arizona slopes upward as you travel north, so that by the time you get to Flagstaff, and the south rim of the canyon, you're well over a mile above sea level. This means that even though you're at roughly the same latitude as South Carolina, March doesn't necessarily mean spring. And I wasn't very enthusiastic about driving a forty-foot bus through a March snowstorm on the Colorado plateau, so we left the RV about a hundred miles north of Phoenix, just off Interstate 17, and headed north in the car. It proved to be a good call.

Here I am contemplating nature on a rock perch about 2,000 feet up. I saw a French guy sitting there as I went by and was so struck by the setting that I offered to take his picture. I then gingerly crept out on the rock and he returned the favor.

Here are Molly, Mom, and Ben on the way down. Molly was too short for the mule ride, but after seeing some of the drop-offs, I was glad to be on my own feet.

Molly studies the rule book for Junior Rangers while Mom checks out a poster on the geology of the canyon.

Grand Canyon National Park

Here's Ben on the trail. He's a mad hiker—just takes off and only waits around for us if he has something special to show us. He also enjoys being able to beat me up the hill pretty much all the time. I can still beat him in arm wrestling, but barely.

And this was a surprise—a series of petroglyphs just below the top of Bright Angel trail. We never would have noticed (I was looking down and puffing pretty hard by that point), but a nice lady hiking with us pointed them out.

Surprisingly, only 10% of the visitors to the Grand Canyon ever venture below the rim, and only 1% go all the way to the bottom. We didn't make it all the way down, either, but we had some beautiful hikes part way down on the Bright Angel and South Kaibab trails.

Travel Tip—if you're planning a trip anything like ours, at your first national park or monument, get a Golden Access Pass for $50.00; it gets you in free to any and all national parks or monuments thereafter. It'll pay for itself in the first two weeks.

Early explorers estimated the width of the Colorado River at the bottom to be six feet. They missed—by a factor of fifty; it's more like 300 feet. The canyon is almost exactly one mile deep and the climate is completely different at the bottom. When it was 60 degrees where we were at the rim, it was over 80 at Phantom Ranch down below.

Molly got into the Junior Ranger program at the parks. Earning a badge involves a kind of treasure hunt through the park museum or environs and a project of some kind. Molly's project was to fill a trash bag. We helped her out and she got a cool patch for her jacket.

We do plan to come back—to visit the North Rim and hike all the way down, stay at the bottom for a couple of days, and hike (slowly) out.

What a place! What a trip! And now it was on to Colorado!

The Checklist

If you are an RVer, this is the most important single page in this book. All the rest can be used for kindling or the outhouse, but you should modify this to suit your needs, copy it, laminate it, and hang it somewhere near the driver's seat. If you use it every time you start up, you'll avoid both embarrassment and expense. If you ignore it, I guarantee you'll pull out one morning leaving the electrical cord attached, if you're lucky. If you're not lucky, it will be something that will make you wish it were the electrical cord.

1. Outside the Rig:

    a. check tire pressure (all around)

    b. unhook and stow all umbilicals (sewer, water, electrical)

    c. check the oil level (about once a month)

    d. check battery water level (about once every two months)

    e. roll in the awning (and be sure it's locked closed)

    f. check the towed vehicle connections

    g. check the vicinity of the rig for obstacles to pulling out cleanly—check high <u>and</u> low

2. Inside the Rig:

    a. pull in and lock slide-outs

    b. crank down and lock TV antenna

    c. stow (or velcro) anything that can fall off a counter or table top

    d. review the route for the day

    e. check the side-view mirrors

    f. start the engine and check fuel level and air-pressure gauges

The Big Circle
Colorado, Arizona, and Back to New Mexico

5

Cliff Houses, Big Houses, and Almost to the Four Corners

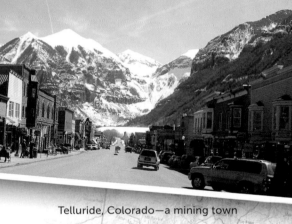

Telluride, Colorado—a mining town where the wealthy are now putting gold back into the ground. Go figure.

We left the Grand Canyon on a snowy Sunday afternoon, headed east through Navajo country toward the Four Corners—the point where Arizona, Colorado, New Mexico, and Utah meet. After taking a short detour north into Monument Valley—driving through everything from hail to bright sunshine—we reached the Four Corners monument, almost, at about 5:15. I say almost because the hundred-yard road to the monument was closed and locked tight at 5:00 p.m. So you just have to imagine a picture of the four of us, each standing in a different state. I would have been in Arizona.

We spent that night in the nice little town of Cortez, Colorado, where Molly and I went to a movie (*Agent Cody Banks*, a kind of Disney James Bond, where the kids save the world from the bad guys as well as their incompetent parents) and Mary found a really cool potter.

The next morning, we had one of those unexpected treats that made the trip so much fun: a stop at Mesa Verde National Park, another gem.

Here are Mom and Ben in front of Tree House at Mesa Verde. The buildings use every inch of the natural cliff overhang and are almost completely protected from the weather, which probably explains why they're still in such amazingly good shape.

Guess who took this picture? Does the fact that his little sister barely made it into the frame give you a hint?

All my life, I've seen pictures of Native American cliff dwellings and been mildly interested; Mary, on the other hand, has always been fascinated with them and was the one to insist that we stop at Mesa Verde. On the way north in Arizona, we had visited a spectacular site called Montezuma's Castle, but it was high on the cliff face and could only be seen at a distance. But in Mesa Verde, we were able to walk right into the cliff houses themselves (albeit under the watchful eye of the park ranger), which was an amazing experience. Built more than a thousand years ago, and then abandoned (for reasons nobody knows) before the Europeans came, these architectural marvels are both fascinating and haunting.

None of us had ever skied in the west, so we decided that this trip gave us the perfect opportunity to try. The only question was where. Through a combination of geography, ski-area policy, and contacts through friends, we ended up in Telluride, Colorado. The geography involved our already being at the Grand Canyon, which is a lot closer to Telluride (on the west side of the Rockies) than Vail or Aspen. Ski-area policy kept us away from Alta, in Utah, or Taos, in New Mexico, since neither allowed snowboarders, of which Ben is most definitely one.

My two favorite girls and the Tree House. Molly is now a Junior Ranger at both the Grand Canyon and Mesa Verde.

(I find this "skiers only" policy pretty bizarre since the only growth in the industry in the last ten years has been in snowboarders. Although I'm a skier, this seems like rank snobbism, and a lousy business decision to boot.)

Finally, we have a friend in Maine who has a sister in Telluride whose brother-in-law books ski accommodations, so that settled it; Telluride it was. And what a beautiful, though somewhat strange, place. It's the only town I've ever been in where there are more real-estate offices than restaurants (or any other business, for that matter).

The skiing was great—huge mountain, no lift lines, good snow, and a tremendous variety of trails. The town itself was interesting, as well, in that it has a real history apart from skiing. In the late nineteenth century, it was a wide-open mining town that had boomed along with similar spots all over the west (such as Bisbee, Arizona). Then the mines closed and the town was on its way to ghost status (there're plenty of them in the west as well) when, in 1972, the ski area was originally developed.

At one point, we saw an "Open House" sign at the edge of a trail and, since Mary and I are both real-estate voyeurs, we went in for a look. The house was about five years old and a fairly good size, but nothing spectacular; nothing spectacular, that is, except the price—$3.9 million. The punch line is that while we were there, a local contractor came by to look it over as a candidate for renovation. He said he thought it had a lot of "potential." In other words, a $3.9 million fixer-upper. Wow.

There were dozens like these all over the mountain; all I could think of were the huge "cottages" the robber barons built in Newport and Bar Harbor at the turn of the last century. I consider myself a thorough-going capitalist, but still found this a bit much.

This, I kid you not, is one house. It has to be at least 8,000 square feet. All for a part-time home. Ben was convinced it was a hotel.

Upon leaving Telluride, we took a five-hour loop through the Rockies, first west, then north, and finally back south to the town of Durango, near the New Mexico border. Looking at this shot, taken from the car, Molly said the mountains looked painted on, and she was right.

About half way through this loop, we came upon the town of Ouray, surrounded on all sides by incredible peaks and containing at its heart this natural hot springs—open to the public year-round.

As I said, the skiing was good, but I think the much-touted vast difference in snow quality between the West and the East is somewhat overrated. I'm sure this perception dates back to the 1950s and 60s (about the time I was learning to ski in New Hampshire), when conditions in the East really were pretty bad at least half the time. Now, however, with the tremendous improvement in snow-making and grooming, places like Sugarloaf in Maine (especially with guys like Crusher directing the groomers) can more than hold their own. We had fun, but we're still unabashed Sugarloafers.

It didn't take Mom and Molly long to get in while Ben and I just soaked up the sun. Molly had to take a swimming test to be allowed to swim in the deep end, which she passed with flying colors.

Angus King 87

And then it was on to Durango for some Serious Texas Bar BQ (that was the name of the restaurant—they even had a letter of endorsement from legendary Texas football coach Darrell Royall). We slept at a Best Western (remember, the RV was still in Arizona—we would be picking it up the next week), then spent a day exploring and shopping—we all got cowboy belts—before driving south back into New Mexico.

Back to New Mexico—Art, the El Rey, and the Lady Lobos

OK, so maybe you've noticed that our route through and around the southwest was a little strange—Texas into southern New Mexico, west to southern Arizona, up to the top of Arizona (the Grand Canyon), up farther to Colorado, then back down into New Mexico (again), over to Arizona (again), and then up into Utah. On the map, it's a big spiral—and it made perfect sense, if you'd been watching the Weather Channel as we were.

Basically, except for the skiing at Telluride, we were trying to stay where it was warm, so we did southern Arizona and New Mexico first in order to give Santa Fe and the canyon country in Arizona and Utah a chance to warm up. And except for a one-day snowstorm in Santa Fe (hey, no plan is perfect), it worked.

Ben standing in between two courtyards in the Martinez Hacienda in Taos, a beautifully preserved adobe farmhouse built in 1804 by a wealthy Spanish merchant.

The hacienda dining room; notice how spare it is—nothing on the walls, simple furniture, and not much light. Metal was so rare in those days that Señor Martinez's will specified the location and disposition of every nail in the place.

We had a long drive south and east from Durango to Taos, the last eighty miles or so on narrow mountain roads in the dark. But Taos was worth it—a stunning landscape, great architecture, and probably the best art per capita in America.

Here's a bit about my driving style, which became an issue in the course of this particular trip. Once we get underway (whether in the car or the RV), I don't like to stop. Period. The other bit of information—maybe more than you need—is that the Good Lord gave me a larger-than-normal capacity to hold liquids (how's that for delicate locution?). My troopers used to suffer mightily from this—because there were never restroom breaks in my days on the road and they'd occasionally have to deputize a passerby to look after me while they…well, you get the idea.

One of our area stops was Bandelier National Monument. The ancient settlement consists of rock rooms reachable by ladders, adobe-style buildings built up against the cliffs, and what can only be called an apartment complex on the valley floor.

Here's Molly on one of the series of ladders that got us up the sheer cliff face. All these ancient sites had a sense of mystery and spiritualism about them; there's something moving about walking among the spirits of long-lost peoples.

Our favorite find in Taos was this open-air antiques dealer that featured doors. Church doors, castle doors, palace doors from India, mansion doors, huge gates; it was a treasure trove of ancient, rough, and often beautiful doors. I couldn't help wonder at the story each might have told—of monks and knights, dark princes and cold castle afternoons.

A simple gate into the courtyard of the El Rey Inn; there was an award for maintenance in the El Rey trophy case—see why?

The nicest hot tub I've ever run across. With the stars out, the fireplace lit, and the water hot, this is a pretty nice place to end a day. Hey, who said it had to be all work?

On this particular drive, the natives in the back seat started to get a little restless about an hour in. "Next gas station," I assured them—and I meant it, I really did. The only problem was that in southwestern Colorado, at eight o'clock at night, there isn't much in the way of gas stations, or anything else, for that matter. So on we went, with the muffled complaints growing louder and more insistent from all quarters (by this time, Mary was among the aggrieved). Finally (and they all put a great deal of emphasis on the "finally"—I still hear about this incident to this day), I pulled over and everybody ran to the bushes. It all came out well (sorry), however, because the spot I pulled over turned out to be right next to a really cool bridge over a dramatic gorge. Actually, I planned it all along.

Like Santa Fe, Taos is a place that blends three cultures—Native American, Spanish, and Anglo—and all three show up in everything from the art to the food.

Mary fell in love with the adobe style. A friend in Maine suggested that it would be perfect for Brunswick, particularly in March—finally, a commercial use for mud season.

Ben really wanted an enormous set of wooden gates that looked like something out of *Young Frankenstein.* We finally convinced him that they would be a little much on Potter Street.

On the way from Taos to Santa Fe, we came across an amazing place called Bandelier National Monument. A friend in Maine had told us it was a "don't miss" in New Mexico, and he was right. This was another great example of the "no itinerary" theory of coast-to-coast travel. If we had been on a schedule, we never would have stopped and would have missed a real treat.

Bandelier lies in a protected valley between huge rock formations that look just like Swiss cheese. About twelve hundred years ago, the holes in the cheese became the homes of a mysterious group of people called the Anasazi ("the ancient ones" in the Navajo language), who populated the valleys and canyons of the southwest until they abruptly disappeared about 1300 AD.

Here again, as at Mesa Verde, we were allowed to actually climb into some of the rooms—you could still see the smoke residue on the ceilings. Mary and I both had the feeling that some day in the not-too-distant future this extraordinary access will no longer be allowed, probably because some bozo won't be able to resist the temptation to carve his initials on the wall.

Molly in the Santa Fe Children's Museum. She is standing inside a circle of soapy water and the hula hoop has surrounded her with a huge bubble.

Mom and Molly thread their way through the canyon at Tent Rocks.

A shot straight up a natural groove at Tent Rocks National Monument between Santa Fe and Albuquerque. Ben wanted to climb it, but I was the spoilsport, and said no. The neatest thing about this place was a narrow winding canyon that looked like something out of *Indiana Jones*—800-foot cliffs ten feet apart at the bottom.

And here's Mom taking a picture of me taking a picture of Mom taking a picture of me. Got it?

Two of Mary's cousins we visited in Albuquerque, Dan Cosper and Kathy Salzstein. The closest I could come to understanding the relationship is that they all have a great-grandfather in common. Nice people.

A somewhat rare moment of familial affection.

In Santa Fe, Mary's guidebook research paid off again in the form of a wonderful place called the El Rey Inn. The El Rey was built in the 1930s, and has been thoughtfully expanded and beautifully maintained ever since. It is as good an example of the charms of "commercial adobe" as we had run across.

During the trip, Ben and Molly acted as perfectly normal twelve- and nine-year-old siblings—in other words, constantly at each other and often driving their parents to the edge (and sometimes over the edge) of distraction. Having said that, we got along amazingly well. The kids grumbled (trolley tours and hikes weren't big favorites, for example, at least not after the first five), but generally went along with our plans more willingly than I would have thought possible. We even caught them being nice to each other every now and then, especially when they didn't think we were watching. We may have been getting to the limit of their canyon tolerance right about the second run through New Mexico, but tough, they'd forget all about it by the time we hit San Diego.

Santa Fe, of course, is a major art center with galleries and museums on every corner. The galleries are generally very high-end (some looked more like museums than commercial establishments) and we sure didn't find any bargains. I liked the museums where you could just rent the good stuff—for sixteen bucks, for example, we had the run of a fabulous Georgia O'Keeffe collection for a couple hours. We just couldn't take it home with us.

Ben couldn't get over the porcelain urinal turned on its side ("Fountain") or the snow shovel on the wall (by Marcel Duchamp) in the O'Keeffe: "This isn't art," quoth he. And, of course, he was right.

On a trip like this, you pick up tips from all kinds of sources. I already mentioned Mary's penchant for guidebooks, which came in handy more than once, but we were also always on the alert for ideas from fellow travelers (unfortunate phrase), especially those with kids. One stop between Santa Fe and Albuquerque (one of my accomplishments of this trip was that I ended up being able to spell Albuquerque without looking it up or asking Mary) was at a new national monument called Tent Rocks we heard about from a family we met at Bandelier, and we heard about Bandelier from a friend back in Maine.

Albuquerque was an important destination for us from the very beginning of the trip. For one thing, Mary has three cousins living there, one of whom she grew up with in Milwaukee. Secondly, one of those cousins was the designated Southwest mail drop for assorted "Correspondence and Important Papers." (You may have wondered how we handled this practical problem of prolonged travel—a friend in Brunswick

Saturday night in Albuquerque—one of the games of the women's Sweet Sixteen, the Lady Lobos of New Mexico against the Red Raiders of Texas Tech. Dick Mann, an old friend of Mary's from Milwaukee (not a cousin), had tickets and we all got to enjoy the spectacle.

The first morning in Santa Fe, we went to the excellent New Mexico Museum of Natural History. There were lots of neat displays on dinosaurs, geology, and astronomy. Cool stuff, as you can see by Molly's expression.

And what do you do if you're nine and find yourself in a motel room with a pair of double beds? Jump from bed to bed, of course.

sorted the mail and sent on what couldn't be taken care of by e-mail or a call, as well as a smattering of magazines.)

Albuequerque has a sensational tram ride—a little pricey ($15 round trip —but it was the best view we found that didn't involve a lot of climbing. Albuquerque went from a population of 85,000 people around 1960 to 600,000 today, which is pretty typical of the Southwest. The problems are traffic and water, with the latter looming as a mega-problem for the whole region in the near future.

And then we headed back into Arizona, this time to the northeastern corner and one of the most extraordinary places in the country, Canyon de Chelly.

For the first time in about forty years, I found myself on a horse, following these three and our Navajo guide into the incredible Canyon de Chelly. The horses were Mary's idea and it was a good one. There was something about their pace and rhythm that was just right for this time and place.

The kids absolutely fell in love with the horses. By the end of the day, they were galloping along (and through) the river—no mean feat for Molly, since her feet didn't even reach the stirrups. I still don't know how she stayed on.

Canyon de Chelly—Unhorsed Yet Unbowed

The mythologist Joseph Campbell calls Canyon de Chelly (pronounced "de Shay") the most sacred place on earth. It is the ancestral home of the Navajo people, and the Anasazi people before them. Hidden in the northeastern corner of Arizona, it is a place that inspires awe and introspection. It's not anywhere near as big as the Grand Canyon, but has a special beauty, based in part on its extraordinary physical presence and in part on its tragic and ultimately triumphant history.

We drove west from Albuquerque on Interstate 40 until we crossed back into Arizona and immediately turned north into the high desert. After a night at the Thunderbird Lodge, we were ready to explore the canyon, but decided not to take the usual Jeep or van tour, but to go in the old-fashioned way.

Not surprisingly, our horses had minds of their own. When they wanted a drink, they stopped and took one. On the way into the canyon, they were

You're not allowed to enter the canyon without a Navajo guide; this is Kee Chee Anagal, who was born and raised in the canyon and introduced us to some of its secrets.

Everywhere you go in the Southwest, you see images of Kokopelli, the flute player, who is the Anasazi god of fertility. He's in gift shops, bars, and motel lobbies, on rugs, pottery, and billboards. But here he is, for real. Looking at these, Ben announced that this must be Kokopelli's home because he's lying down, presumabley asleep.

Mary and Kee on the way into the canyon. She has an absolutely extraordinary way of making friends with people and it enriched this trip again and again. She is genuinely warm and people can sense it—so we end up with local contacts and knowledge that would otherwise be impossible.

Think Molly had a good time?

Here's Mary at one of the overlooks. Finally, we had some warm days.

slow and a little balky, but as soon as we turned around to head out (and back to their stables and their lunch), they picked up the pace considerably.

Or in the case of my horse, Checkers, a little too considerably. So here's what happened; ignore whatever you hear from my disloyal kids.

Checkers decided he wanted to get back sooner than the rest of us had planned, so he suddenly took off at a brisk pace. Not a gallop, exactly, but more than a trot. Not wanting to leave Mary and the kids behind (sure, Angus), I applied the brakes in the form of a loud "whoa" and a rather vigorous tug on the reins—too vigorous, as it turned out.

This gives you an idea of the scale of the place; at the bottom is a river, farms, and grazing land.

Checkers did as he was told and stopped on a dime. The problem was, I didn't. Applying the principles of Newton's First Law of Motion ("A body, once placed in motion, will remain in motion until acted upon by an outside force"), which Ben and I had been studying, I flew gracefully (?) over Checkers' head, did a neat tuck and roll, and landed unceremoniously on the bank of the river, still clutching the reins, which I had somehow managed to pull off the horse as I flew over. This meant, of course, that Checkers was now free to return home at his own pace, which he proceeded to do, leaving me with the prospect of a three-mile walk.

Fortunately, our friend Kee was prescient in such matters and had come equipped with a lasso (the first one I had ever seen in person), and he took off after Checkers, returning a few minutes later with the wayward horse in tow. And what did I do? I followed Newton's other famous principle applicable in such cases—I Got Back on the Horse, and we made it back without further incident.

Needless to say, the kids loved the whole incident and there was much good-natured (dare I say it?) horseplay about it for the next couple of days. There's nothing any kid enjoys more than seeing Dad humbled; they sure got it in this case.

That night, Mary and I brought the kids dinner from the lodge cafeteria and left them in the tender embrace of the Disney Channel (*Zenon: the Zequel*) while we had a rare night out to plan the next few days.

Since we had been down to the canyon floor, the next day we drove the rim and stopped at a series of breathtaking overlooks.

Outside a traditional Navajo hogan. These can still be seen scattered across Indian Country.

We passed through this town on the way back—there's got to be a story here.

Mary and Molly with Marlys Parks, the wonderful proprietress of the Krazy K, where we left the RV on our way to the Grand Canyon, and Telluride and New Mexico.

While at the canyon, I remembered that when we were in Taos, we had visited the museum/home of the famous scout and frontiersman Kit Carson. There were a lot of artifacts and stories about his life on display. One element of all of the narratives was something to the effect that Kit Carson was really a friend to the Indians, despite bad press to the contrary. I noticed when I read several of these disclaimers that there was a little of the "Methinks she doth protest too much" quality to them.

I found out when I got to Canyon de Chelly that I was right. In 1864, on the orders of the territorial governor, Kit Carson led a force of soldiers through the canyon, burned the farms and homes, and literally drove the Navajos out. The 8,000 who survived were then forced to march 300 miles to a detention camp in southern New Mexico—several thousand more died along the way. The Navajo people still refer to this as "The Long Walk." They were held in New Mexico for four years before being allowed to return to their ancestral home in the canyon.

But return they did, and after many years managed to rebuild their society, to the point that the Navajos are now our largest single Native American tribe. Their weaving is in such demand that a 3- x 6-foot handwoven rug sells for more than $2,000. Their lot is still not easy, but at least they now control the canyon that is so much a part of their history and lives.

I will always remember the drive back to Camp Verde, where we had left the RV, both because of its variable beauty (we passed through incredible desert, as

This is Spider Rock in the south end of the canyon; you really can't get the scale, but I'd guess the taller spire is at least eight hundred feet high. You can see the river that meanders through the canyon bottom to the left center.

Do your kids ever drive you (almost) over the edge?

well as high-elevation forest near Flagstaff) and also because on the way, we listened to the moving autobiography of one of Mary's heroes, Hank Aaron.

Hearing Aaron's stories about minor league baseball in the south in the early 1950s was a shocking reminder to me (I grew up in Virginia around the same time) and a revelation to the kids. What Jackie Robinson, Aaron, Larry Doby, and dozens of other black ball players of that period put up with seems unbelievable to us today. The story ends with Aaron's dogged pursuit of Babe Ruth's homerun record. The bad part was the content of the hate mail he received (I'm sure the kids had never heard much of the language); the good part was the more than 900,000 pieces of congratulatory mail that came in during the same period.

I came away from the book with a lot of respect for a superlative ball player, but even more for the character of an extraordinary man.

We finally made it back to the Dutch Star at the Krazy K RV Park in Camp Verde. And after almost three weeks in motels and restaurants, we were delighted to be "home." ◈

Perspective

One of my favorite images in all of literature is from Douglas Adams' classic *The Hitchhiker's Guide to the Galaxy*. The image is of the most sinister and diabolical torture machine ever devised—the Total Perspective Vortex. Resembling nothing more scary than an old-fashioned phone booth (have you noticed that these familiar objects of our youth have all but disappeared?), once inside, the occupant is confronted in blazing clarity with his or her true significance in the vastness of the universe.

Ouch.

The concept of perspective, in its very essence, involves where you are standing when you look at something and how your vantage point affects what you see and experience. With the occasional exceptions of governors' conferences and trade missions to other countries, my perspective while in office was entirely focused upon Maine as the center of the universe.

Our coast was more beautiful, our people harder working and more virtuous, our trees taller, and our children all above average, to borrow the line from Garrison Keillor. But most importantly, from my point of view, our challenges were bigger than in other states— our taxes were higher, our regulations more onerous, our power more expensive, our rural areas were in greater decline, and only our children were leaving.

At least that's what I thought until I saw thirty-three other states from the inside. What I found were shuttered and empty stores on the main streets of fishing villages in Oregon (not unlike the Down East coast of Maine); rural towns in South Dakota that had lost their high school to regional consolidation (just like some of our formerly thriving lumber towns in northern Maine); headlines lamenting the flight of young people to glittering cities nearby, whether Boise, Chicago, Minneapolis, or (in our case) Boston. And, there was universal aggravation over the depredations of the local politicians, whatever their party or political philosophy.

This struck me particularly in Washington State, which I found to

be much like Maine. In Maine, one of our most persistent problems—dating back at least a hundred years—is what we call the Two Maines: the more prosperous and economically diverse southern part of the state, centered on Portland and its proximity to Boston, and the northern and eastern parts, whose economies have always been based on natural resources—farming, fishing, and forestry—all of which seem to be in a perpetual state of gradual decline. Generations of leaders—governors, legislators, mayors, local citizens—have worked on this, trying everything from special tax incentives, infrastructure improvements, and educational centers to regional industrial parks and development authorities. In fact, I spent the better part of my second term trying to slow, if not reverse, this seemingly inexorable trend.

And, to my surprise, so it was in Washington, only tilted 90 degrees. The western part of the state was where the action was —around Seattle and Tacoma—but the agricultural eastern counties were struggling—and the two regions were in constant competition for state resources and attention. Georgia, New Mexico, Oregon, Louisiana, even California, and virtually every other state we visited was coping with a similar problem in one way or another.

This didn't make Maine's situation any better or easier to bear (there's no sight more poignant to me than a rusted goal post at the end of an abandoned high school football field), but it helped me to understand that it wasn't only *our* problem—and that there were economic, social, and demographic forces at work that were bigger than one state or region.

Perspective won't change your situation, but it can deepen your understanding—and can often suggest solutions. And changing your vantage point—such as by getting out on the road—is what gaining perspective is all about.

6

Utah, Nevada & California

Back in the RV—John Wayne, Hoodoos, and the Sturgis of Jeeps

Mary and I pose in Monument Valley on the Arizona-Utah border. The day we did the Navajo park loop was especially spectacular in that the weather kept changing, from sandstorm to rain to sun to heavy overcast. The "monuments" were even more striking when bathed in patches of sunlight against the moving clouds. This is an amazing place.

If I had to pick one area of the country for sheer physical beauty (after the Maine coast, of course), it would have to be southern Utah. The mountains, high desert, and alpine forests just kept coming at us—various, changeable, surprising, and almost always stunning. Molly kept saying, "It looks like it was painted on."

Monument Valley was a special favorite of the great director of Western movies, John Ford (born Sean Aloysius O'Feeney in Portland, Maine, by the way) and one of Ford's regular actors, John Wayne. We rented one of Ford and Wayne's greatest collaborations, *Stagecoach,* the night we arrived, and the kids could immediately identify the settings. John Wayne went on to star in a number of other movies set here, including *She Wore a Yellow Ribbon,* which we rented the next night (it couldn't touch *Stagecoach*).

Reminds me of the great country song by Confederate Railroad:

> She never cried when Old Yeller died
> She wasn't washed in the blood of the Lamb
> She never stood up for "The Star Spangled Banner"

So what did we do with no Jeep to go off-roading in? We rented a Hummer.

And she wasn't a John Wayne fan
Her baby-blue eyes had the warning signs
That woman was bad to the bone
She never cried when Old Yeller died
So do you think I'll cry when she's gone?

Sheer poetry.

Long before now, I should have mentioned one of our best discoveries of this trip—XM Satellite Radio. For $9.95 a month, we got 100-plus channels of everything from fifties rock to classics to CNN to old-time radio drama, all without having to deal with the frustration of local stations fading in and out as you travel. All of us seemed to like the Fifties Channel, Mary and I because it brought back "So Many Memories" (in fact, that's the name of one of the songs)—although Mary keeps reminding me that she was just a toddler in those days—and the kids just plain like the sound. Ben, for example, has became a big Little Richard fan, insisting that I turn it up whenever "Long Tall Sally" or "Tutti Frutti" came on.

Outside of Moab, Utah, about to drive up a 40% grade on rough bare rock. To put it into perspective, a steep hill where the signs say "Trucks Check Brakes and Use Low Gear" is 8%. It's impossible to shake the sensation that you're about to flip over backwards.

She looks pretty casual here, but wasn't so sure fifteen minutes before. Do you think we can get Friends of Acadia to allow this on Mt. Desert?

Can't you just see John Wayne riding across this scene? He came to the valley often, staying in a cabin behind the Goulding's Lodge, which is still there (and was used as a set in *She Wore a Yellow Ribbon*). The cabin is now part of what is called a museum, but is more like a shrine to Ford and Wayne. We really do love celebrities in this country and they don't get any bigger than Duke.

Angus King 105

Earlier in the day, Mary had been in an outdoors store and, on a whim, got everyone a pedometer. This brought out all our competitive instincts. Here it is at about 10:00 p.m. and Mary and Molly are walking up and down in the RV to pad their totals. On a typical non-driving day, we seemed to average about four miles apiece. No wonder we slept so well.

Here's a shot in Arches National Park. But I have a confession—by about this point, all of us started to get a little "canyoned-out." We'd been in this kind of country for almost a month and it seemed the oohs and aahs were becoming a little scripted. I suppose the same thing happens to tour guides in the Louve.

So you have to get the picture of us driving through this incredible countryside with The Platters, Buddy Holly, The Marvelettes, Marvin Gaye, The Moonlighters, Little Anthony and the Imperials, the Everly Brothers, or James Brown ("The Hardest Working Man in Show Business") on the box. Heaven definitely involves Rock and Roll.

From Monument Valley, we went north and slightly east to the town of Moab, which sits almost exactly halfway between Arches and Canyonlands National Parks.

When we pulled into the RV park in Moab (we'd gotten pretty casual about places to stay by this time; we didn't even call ahead, we just drove into town looking for a likely campground), we noticed two things—1) all our neighbors seemed to be towing Jeeps, and 2) the park was just about

full, which seemed odd this early in the season. We soon found out why, on both counts.

It was the 37th Annual Moab Jeep Safari, and within a few days, something like 10,000 Jeeps were expected in town. So what did we do with no Jeep to go off-roading in? The only logical thing, of course; we rented a Hummer (with an expert driver—not me).

The trail was called Hell's Revenge and wound through the mountains just east of Moab. As we started up the first grade, Molly looked at Matt, the driver, and said—totally seriously—"Have you done this before?" "No," he deadpanned, "I just got my driver's license last week."

It was a wonderful experience; but then, of course, Ben set his heart on getting a Hummer—I think they're pretty cool, myself. The subliminal appeal is knowing you can drive up and over anybody else; it's a guy thing.

That night, we did a local institution—a boat trip up the Colorado at dusk, featuring a dramatic lighting of the canyon walls synchronized with a tape on the history of the region (from the Cretaceous to the Mormons—that's a lot of territory in an hour). The lighting was done by a truck equipped with powerful searchlights driving along the canyon road parallel to the boat. It was really neat.

Mary and Ben with one of their more and more frequent height tests. I make it a dead heat; Mom's toast before we get back to Maine.

Moab is what would have happened if L.L. Bean had invented Disneyland. It is outdoor crazed—Jeeps, hiking, dirt bikes, mountain bikes, you name it. Here is a random shot of a Moab parking lot. I count six mountain bikes and two kayaks, and it's only April.

And guess what? Here we are again, heading down into Bryce Canyon on horseback; only this time, I managed to keep the shiny side up, as we say about our Harleys.

Finally, our last stop in Utah was Bryce Canyon. One of the amazing things about the different canyonscapes we had seen over the last six weeks was the variety. Each had its own shapes, colors, size, and mood. Bryce was no exception—it looked and felt completely different from any of the others, with its strange stone shapes (called "Hoodoos") and brilliant colors. Again, the camera can't do it justice, but here's the idea, lower left.

Nevada to San Diego—The Blue Man Group, A Dam Tour, and the Man in the Panda Suit

Our destination in Nevada was Hoover Dam, but when we arrived at Lake Mead and saw a sign that said Las Vegas, 26 miles—well, what would you have done? So we took off for a Saturday night on The Strip and drove from one end to the other, just taking it all in—the giant, gaudy casinos, the people of all ages, shapes, and sizes, the colors, the drive-thru (no kidding) wedding chapels. If there is a world capital of neon, Las Vegas is it.

Hoodoos at Bryce Canyon.

Ben and Molly concentrate on The Sims on the road to Nevada; I wish I could claim that it's quadratic equations. No, they don't get along this well all that often. (Why do you think we took the picture?)

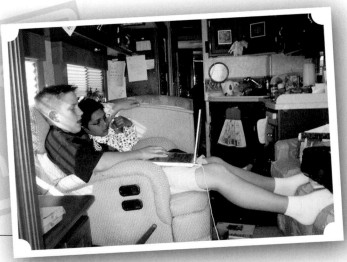

Instead of spending all of our time at Arches or Canyonlands, we took some local advice and visited Dead Horse Point, an area state park. It was a good choice. An incredible place high on a mesa overlooking the Colorado River and the snow-covered LaSalle Mountains, this was one of the most spectacular spots we saw on the whole trip.

Notice that the Blue Man doesn't break character, even for a post-show picture with a young fan. These guys are cool.

Lake Mead—notice the incredibly low water level. The locals said they had never seen it so low (about eighty feet down). The politics of water in the Southwest is something we in the East can only dimly understand, but as the drought continues, the tensions are rising in proportion to the fall in the water levels.

We finally parked at the Luxor (naturally, a giant pyramid) and, on a whim, got some cancellation tickets for the late show of the Blue Man Group.

Before the show, we cruised one end of The Strip—the Luxor, Excaliber, and New York, New York. We didn't gamble—you can walk through the casinos with kids as long as you don't stop at the machines. (We may be the first people to spend an entire evening in Vegas without losing a dime.) The kids played arcade games and Mary and I just watched the action. It got a little depressing after a while, but for sheer spectacle, this was the place.

Then, we went back to the Luxor for the fantastic Blue Man show. We'd seen them in short pieces—remember the Intel commercials?—but never really saw what they do until this memorable night. Their show is a combination of mime, incredible drumming, high-tech theater wizardry, all

This is the scene about forty miles south of Las Vegas. Can anybody seriously argue that we should want this in Maine? Alas, it now looks inevitable.

with an underlying layer of dry humor. It was one of the most amazing entertainment experiences I have ever had. If you're ever in a town where the Blue Man Group is playing, don't miss the show.

The next day we went back to Hoover Dam—definitely worth the trip. Hoover Dam is a true engineering wonder, and the tour was fun, especially the trip down into the powerhouse at the base of the dam. Conceived by Herbert Hoover when he was Secretary of Commerce and begun during his presidency, it was completed in 1935, both for flood control of the Colorado River and the production of electricity. Incidentally, it also created Lake Mead, the largest artificial lake in North America, which is a major recreational amenity for the Las Vegas region.

And who should we meet 500 feet inside the dam? Martha Muldoon and Denise Butler of Kennebunk, Maine. They both work for Joel Stevens at Kennebunk Savings and were in Las Vegas for a bankers' convention. Martha's greeting to me in the elevator was something along the lines of "Gone a little native, Angus?"—must've been the beard.

Here, Ben contemplates the Colorado from near the top of the Hoover Dam.

Our plan was to drive from Las Vegas to San Diego in one day, which looked doable on the map. Only the map failed to note the phenomenon of all the Los Angelenos heading back home from Vegas on Sunday afternoon. (If major casinos ever get to southern California, Las Vegas is in trouble—about 75% of the cars we saw in the casino parking lots were from California.)

We never did see a "Welcome to California" sign like we saw everywhere else; instead, our greeting upon crossing the line was a fifty-mile-long (no joke) traffic jam. The first of several in the Golden State, I might add.

So we stopped for the night in Calico State Park, just outside of Barstow—the first RV park we encountered that was attached to a full-blown ghost town. (Quiz: where was the combination RV park and catfish farm?) The next morning we hung out for a while and enjoyed the attractions (the RV park fee included admission to the ghost town). The big disappointment, however, was that the rain caused the cancellation of the scheduled gunfight. Wouldn't want the gunslingers to slip and fall, I guess.

Then came the worst day of the trip—eight hours of stop-and-go traffic, the last three in driving rain on the freeway around Los Angeles and down to San Diego. It appears that rain is to southern California drivers as snow is to Washingtonians. Cars were off the road, traffic absolutely crawled, and just changing lanes (especially in a forty-foot bus towing a car) was an undertaking of some daring. It was awful; never have I been so glad to see a KOA RV park. In fact, I was eckstatic.

Our first visit in San Diego was the famous zoo. It may be heresy, but I was underwhelmed. The animals were often hard to see, or just plain absent. The biggest problem, however, became apparent as I toured with Molly—many, if not most, of the pens are separated from the walking paths by hedge-like shubbery that is very difficult (in many places impossible) for a kid to see over. This natural separation is a point of pride for the zoo and is no problem for adults, but really limits the visibility of the animals for a kid. Maybe the folks who run the place should do a walk-around with a six-year-old.

The pandas, on the other hand, were really cool. (What do you call it when visitors to this zoo run amok? *Panda*monium, of course.) My only problem was they looked too good; I tried to convince the kids that they were really zoo employees in panda suits; nobody was buying, but I'm not so sure.

The next day, we visited San Diego's other major attraction, Sea-World. Now this was more like it—you could see every animal and it was clearly designed with kids in mind. And the killer whale show was, well, killer.

At the seal pool, you could buy little fish at feeding time (four bucks a box—these guys are no fools). The only problem was if you held the fish out more than a few seconds, one of the aggressive seagulls would fly by and snatch it. This surprised the kids and irritated the seals to no end.

Ben has been a Lego whiz from the age of two, and our house has always been full of the little yellow, red, and blue blocks. (Have you ever stepped on a Lego in bare feet in the middle of the night? The very memory is painful.) And ever since we bought our first box all those years ago, Mary has wanted to go to Legoland in San Diego. So, we went.

C'mon, does this guy look like a bear to you?

Here is the famous Shamu, at San Diego's SeaWorld. If you look closely, there's a man standing on his nose as he rockets out of the water. Wow!

Oops, what's this zoo picture doing here? That was yesterday. Because the elephants are actually made of Legos, by the thousands.

And what about this view of San Francisco? We're not due there for two weeks. More Legos, of course.

Another example of the Lego modellers' art—the San Francisco skyline.

The heart of Legoland is a wonderful series of Lego models of familiar places—Times Square, Mount Rushmore, the Eiffel Tower, the Sydney Opera House, and even a New England seaport (looked a lot like Rockport, Maine, to me). It was fun trying to line up the pictures so they'd look almost like the real thing.

And finally, from San Diego—the second of our three big right turns at the corners of the country—we headed north for the first time. Our next stop was Yosemite, but not before a stop in Bakersfield and a night with Buck Owens and the Buckaroos. Hee haw!

Yosemite, Bakersfield, and San Francisco—Bakersfield?

This is the kind of picture that is hard to resist. This bear stands in the Yosemite Village General Store and my guess is that something close to this pose is snapped by at least half of each year's Yosemite visitors, of which there are about four million.

And therein lies a problem (with the four million, not the bear). More on this later, but first, we had to pass through Bakersfield.

Bakersfield, you see, is a great place to stop for the night when you are trying to drive all the way from San Diego to Yosemite in one day but the lighter plug in your towed car crumps out just as

Well, how's this for a view from the front of the RV? We're in the San Francisco RV Resort and it's like having a million-dollar condo in Malibu.

Lest you think I'm exaggerating, to the left is the view from the windshield. What a spot, and only about twenty minutes from downtown San Francisco.

you are leaving and the Brake Buddy* won't work and your wife has to go and find a mechanic in a strange city who will drop everything and fix it and you finally get going, but not until two hours later, and then it starts to blow about fifty miles an hour and spit rain and you just know you don't want to be climbing into the foothills of the Sierras after dark in the rain driving a forty-foot bus. Whew!

Buck Owens, if you recall, was the co-star of *Hee Haw* in the 70s. (Quiz: Who was the other star, the one who played the banjo?) Well, Buck was still at it when we went through Bakersfield (sadly, he died in 2006), at his own dinner theater, Buck Owens' Crystal Palace. We went in after setting up in

Bakersfield was the home of the estimable Buck Owens (on the right, above), if not each of the Buckeroos.

The Brake Buddy is an ingenious device that sits on the floor of the towed car and automatically applies the car's brakes in proportion to the brakes being applied in the RV, all without a lot of wiring and no messing with the hydraulics of either the car or the RV. But it does need power from the cigarette lighter, and on this particular day, that wasn't going to happen. Mary found the mechanic who not only dropped everything to help us out, but also was downright friendly about the whole thing. If you ever have car trouble in San Diego, Dan at Becka Automotive is your man.

We did have one great hike up the north face of the valley to the base of Upper Yosemite Falls; it was pretty steep (all switchbacks). Here are Mom and Molly taking a breather on the way up.

the KOA north of town and most of us (see below) had a great time. We heard some good country music ("I've Got a Tiger By the Tail" was Buck's signature tune) and were even moved to dance a couple times. This latter was too much for Ben, who literally hid his head inside his jacket. "It wasn't the music," he said. "It was the old people dancing."

Then, it was on to Yosemite. The drive up California Route 140 from Merced to Yosemite was one of the most beautiful we had—not dramatic like Utah—but lovely, with grassy, rolling hills, grazing cattle, and gradually steeper grades until we reached the small towns of Mariposa, Midpines, and finally El Portal, right outside the park. Unfortunately, we didn't have great weather for our visit and only saw Yosemite Valley shrouded in clouds and lazy mists. But it's still a wonderful place.

Yosemite is one of the most beautiful and moving places on earth; a hidden valley carved by glaciers with dramatic sheer cliffs and waterfalls at every turn. Its problem is one I've mentioned before—it's simply overwhelmed by too many visitors. We were there in mid-April, not the high summer season (although it was school vacation in parts of California), and it still felt like Kennebunkport in August. Tour buses, lines at the store, endless circling for a parking place, and hikes where you pass someone (or, in my case, they pass you) every five minutes—not exactly the stuff of solitude and the contemplation of nature. I couldn't imagine what it must be like in July.

To its credit, the Park Service is wrestling with this issue on an on-going basis and clearly understands the conflict inherent in its basic charge—to make America's natural wonders accessible while at the same time preserving and protecting them for future generations. There's no easy answer to this one, but some steps seem pretty obvious, like getting the cars out of at least some of the parks altogether and using shuttle buses or some other alternative. It seems to me that something like this has to come—at least to the more crowded parks—in the pretty near future.

One of the best parts of our visit to Yosemite was connecting with Phoebe Hazard, daughter of Bruce and Wendy Hazard, old friends from Belgrade, Maine. At the time, Phoebe was an outdoor experience instructor with the Yosemite Institute, which works with middle- and high-school groups that come to the park for week-long stays. It's always fun to have someone with local knowledge providing advice, and Phoebe gave us a great short course on Yosemite, if only for our next visit. She's a terrific kid and has that wonderful Hazard smile, as you can see.

Yosemite is full of streams, especially at this time of year, all running into the Merced River, which, along with the glaciers, was the architect of the valley. Molly and Ben swore it was warm, trying to get me to jump in; I knew better. I keep telling them that I was born at night, but it wasn't last night.

One of the jewels of Yosemite isn't a waterfall or day hike, however, it's the Ahwahnee, the classic old hotel on one edge of the valley. Built in the 1920s, the common spaces—like its wonderful reading room—have a special grace and unpretentious charm characteristic of the great lodges of the West. We learned that you can experience and enjoy these places by

I thought the windmills were so cool, in fact, that after returning to Maine, I got into the windpower business, but its tough; everybody's for progress, nobody's for change.

And, of course, we had to visit Alcatraz.

having a meal in the dining room (or a Coke in the bar in this case), which is considerably less expensive than staying in one of the rooms.

San Francisco isn't that far from Yosemite (which may be one of Yosemite's problems) and on the way, we saw an amazing sight—electricity-producing windmills on all sides of the pass. We couldn't count them all, but there seemed like at least a thousand, all silently turning against the blue of the sky. They looked cool.

It's hard to know where to start on a visit to the Bay Area, but our great location in Pacifica, just south of San Francisco, allowed us to see sights (and friends) both in the city and to the south, in Silicon Valley.

One of the local sights, of course, is Alcatraz; I couldn't help thinking what it must have been like to see this sight knowing you might never leave the island once the boat docked. The island was only a federal prison for about thirty years (1934–63), but its forbidding image is indelibly imprinted on America's consciousness.

The next day was one of the most exciting of the whole trip (I know because the kids told me so). We had the extraordinary opportunity of visiting Skywalker Ranch, the home of George Lucas' far-flung movie enterprise. George Lucas is vitally interested in education and established a foundation to support educational reform, especially in the area of technology. They had contacted me the previous winter about Maine's 7th-grade computer initiative—they liked it—and mentioned the possibility of visiting the ranch when we were in the area (it's about thirty miles north of San Francisco). We didn't have to be asked twice.

And, amazingly, we got to meet George Lucas himself, who was, as truly great people usually are, completely unpretentious and approachable. In my experience, the really first-rate talents are usually pretty normal; it's the second-tier celebrities who tend to be prima donnas.

What do you say when you meet George Lucas, the creator of the *Star Wars* saga and Indiana Jones, as well as the father of the modern marriage of technology and movie making? After some thought, I told him that, sure, I liked *Star Wars,* but my favorite of his movies was *American Graffiti* because it so perfectly captured the feel of my high school experience in the sixties. Turns out, this was a great opener, because, as it happened, both of us graduated from high-school in the same year and it was that year he immortalized in *Graffiti.* Did you know that Suzanne Somers was the girl in the T-bird?

So, Alcatraz, the Exploratorium, the Transamerica Pyramid; what was left? Ghirardelli Square, of course, for chocolate, ice cream, and a silly hat for Molly. Alas, about the only thing we missed was a cable car ride, but we had to save something for next time.

On Sunday, we drove (the car) south to visit our friend Josh Stern from Brunswick, who was then a first-year student at Stanford. What an incredible place to spend four years. At the heart of the new economy in any region of the country is a knowledge factory, and Stanford in many ways is the parent of Silicon Valley.

I had visited this area several times in recent years and the change from when I was there in 2000—at the height of the tech boom—was

Here is Molly in front of the main house at Skywalker Ranch, which serves as a sort of corporate headquarters.

As close as I'll get to an Oscar, but Molly, on the other hand...

I had never been emotional about trees; having lived most of my life in Maine, I always valued the forest, but assumed a certain level of harvesting as being part of the natural order of things. But the California redwoods were different—in size, age, and sheer presence. For the first time, I could understand why these trees have been the center of so much controversy.

amazing. Far less traffic, smaller crowds on the streets of the city, and miles of vacant buildings all were noticeable symptoms of the drastic fall of the technology sector in the ensuing three years. It has come back, but the transformation was an object lesson of the dangers of having all your economic eggs in one basket. Thank goodness I wasn't more successful in my efforts to bring some of these now-non-existent jobs to Maine. Lesson: Be careful what you wish for.

And finally, we were headed north, across the Golden Gate Bridge after a somewhat harried drive through downtown San Francisco.

North of San Francisco

As we drove north of San Francisco, everything about California seemed to change—the towns got smaller, the traffic (mercifully) lightened up, and there was much more of a middle America sense to the countryside. Willits, a small town about a hundred miles up the coast, felt about as far from Los Angeles as Brunswick, Maine.

One important note about the geography of the west coast—it's easy to drive north and south, but forget trying to go west to east along the way. It's the mountains, see, and what few east-west roads there are all have these little dots beside them on the map, which the legend says means "scenic route" but really means "only a complete idiot would try to drive a forty-foot RV on this twisty, up-one-side-of-the-mountain-and-down-the-other road."

In fact, our *Professional Drivers' RoadAtlas,* which shows truck routes in every state, didn't identify a single east-west route in California north of San Francisco.

Because we were headed for Eureka, on the northern California coast, to see Mary's cousin, Tony Weiner, we missed the interior valleys and much of the famous wine country. But we saw something even more impressive—the giant redwoods of the northern California coast.

I realize that I'm treading on dangerous ground here, but somehow the idea of cutting down something that took five hundred years to grow (there are some more than 2,000 years old) just doesn't seem right. It's like we're taking something away in our one measly generation that doesn't really belong to us. By the way, we're doing the same thing with oil. It took millions of years to make and we're going to use it up in about 150 years. Reminds me of the old saying—pigs get fat, but hogs get slaughtered.

I still believe in the use of trees (don't worry, I haven't become a druid)—for lumber, paper, and as a legitimate source of jobs and economic development—but maybe there should be a distinction between those that

The days we were in this area were rainy—they'd had ten inches in a week—and mudslides had closed roads in all directions. Here's one that had just been cleaned up.

Molly at the edge of a rain-swollen stream amid the redwoods.

Of course, no trip in and among the redwoods would be complete without a drive-through tree. This one at a private park in Leggett, California, is more than 300 feet tall and about 2,000 years old.

And finally, we got to Eureka, had a great visit with Tony and his puppy Mitch, and visited Ferndale, a wonderfully preserved Victorian town where Molly found this life-size doll house.

can come back in a single generation (like the spruce-fir forest of the Northeast) and these giants, which take hundreds of years to mature.

From Willits, we drove (in the car) through the redwoods west to the coast and found a beautiful beach in a little town called Fort Bragg.

The only thing is, the ocean is on the wrong side; isn't it just like Californians to arrange for sunsets over the ocean instead of having to wake up 5:00 a.m. like we do to get the same view?

And then we came around a corner and could have sworn we were back in Maine (except for that ocean-on-the-wrong-side thing). We were in Mendocino, a town that looks so much like New England that they filmed *Murder, She Wrote* here instead of in Maine, where it was supposed to be. (Boy, did Maine people get a hoot out of the pitiful attempts at Down East accents in that show.)

The day we were in Mendocino, there was an antique sports car rally going on and the place was full of amazing cars—Ferraris, vintage Porsches, Jags, and this beauty that I couldn't identify, except that it was Italian and gorgeous.

At Fort Bragg, Molly and Ben explored and built sand castles while Mom couldn't resist a nap in the sun.

This unique sculpture—called *Time and The Maiden*—is on top of the Masonic Hall (now a bank) on Mendocino's main street. It was supposedly carved from a single piece of redwood back in the 1880s.

Big moment—the first trimming of "The Beard." I was starting to feel more like Gabby Hayes than Sean Connery, so dropped into Mitch's Barber Shop on the main corner of Mendocino. You've got to love a town that has a barber shop in its equivalent of Times Square.

The kids, however, were less impressed and started to "ooh-ahh" derisively whenever we got carried away by the views. Little darlin's.

We then headed north towards Eureka to see Mary's cousin Tony (whom I've known for years, as well). Along the way, we got a taste of the northern California-Oregon coast, which is right up there with Maine's (and for me, that's saying a lot). The difference is that where Maine has wooded and rocky islands, they have just plain rocks. It's an entirely different feel— wild, somewhat threatening, yet really beautiful.

Driving along this narrow highway was a little exciting; the secret was to just take our time and remember to pull over every now and then and let the people behind us pass. It seemed that everyone we talked to before the trip had a "stuck behind an RV" story, so I was ultra-conscious of not being an obstruction. Fortunately, the road builders out there put in lots of pull-over spaces for just such occasions.

Next, the final right turn. ✦

We saw this rainbow on the way back to Willits from Mendocino; it's just spectacular country. Mary and I have been non-stop overwhelmed by the constantly changing landscape we experienced over the past four months.

Mary's shot through the RV window—three views of the coast in one shot.

A WORD FROM MOM

I still keep in my desk the scrap of paper Angus and I scratched out one snowy day in the winter of 1998. It was a Five Year Plan impulsively written when I needed to know when I would be able to stop worrying about things like whether or not I had lipstick on when I went to the grocery store or what bumper stickers I had on my car. So much about life in the public eye was wonderful, exciting, and challenging, but I longed for more family time and, especially, a little anonymity.

Part of the background here is that since childhood I've loved life on the road. I have the warmest (literally, because it was before auto air conditioning) memories of driving to visit my father's parents in Sandusky, Ohio, each summer and can practically recite the (yes, I *am* that old) Burma Shave ads along the way. No seatbelts, rolling around in the flattened back seat area of my parents Country Squire station wagon, it's amazing my brothers and I are still alive. Since those days, I've always loved the relaxation, the change of pace, the sights, and mostly time with family that a road trip entails. I still remember portions of trip logs, ongoing family jokes, and the wonder of vending machines along the Pennsylvania Turnpike.

Equally alluring were photos of old-time "auto-campers," usually homemade, or early Airstreams and Winnebagos. I loved the idea of life pared down to its simplest: narrow beds, a cramped bathroom, tiny kitchen, and mini-refrigerators: "playing house" while on the road.

So these ideas came together for our trip—time to catch up with family, regain a little privacy, and return to the road of my childhood. I knew better than anyone that it would be nearly impossible for Angus to wake up the morning after leaving office and know what to do with himself. The momentum brought on by eight years (actually ten, with two years of campaigning) of non-stop challenges, four-per-hour meetings and

appointments, three-per-day speeches, starched shirts, dark suits, polished shoes, overseas trade missions (cultural lessons included), meetings, meetings, meetings, would be hard to stop. We would definitely need to "Get Outta Dodge" (well, Augusta and Brunswick), re-group as a family, re-acquaint in a relaxed environ-ment . . . and just have some *fun* together.

Thus was born The Plan—which would also be the beginning of the next chapter of our lives. The winter of 2003 felt far away at that point, but "RV Trip" was at least penciled in.

Fast-forward to January 9, 2003 and we were finally, truly, and literally "On The Road," sent off by that wonderful and still-mysterious-of-origin "Thank You For 8 Great Years" sign. All that morning, I was packing boxes and sweeping rooms and probably would still be at it, but the kids finally shouted "Let's go!" and we were off. I left the mess to good friends, donned my cowboy hat, and ahhhh . . .

What I loved most about the trip was the unlimited, unending time with family. There was something about the lack of deadlines and schedules that made the time together seem so open-ended and precious; it was a quality of time that we had never experienced and one that I suspect is pretty rare in any family these days.

My vision was to do the perimeter of the country, clockwise, heading for national and state parks, forests and monuments, friends and family. Angus was astonished at the number of family members I was able to plug into our very loose schedule. He balked initially at all the stops I wanted to make, but it turned out that these breaks from in-RV life that were spent in the living rooms, kitchens, and backyards of old friends and distant cousins turned out to be very important for all of us. Ben and Molly interacted with other kids and got a break from us, and we got to talk to actual grown-ups.

Once on the road, I appointed myself Trip Guide and Cruise Director. In those pre-Wi-Fi days, I sat the kids down each evening—or morning—and delivered the

guidebook's description of our next destination. I can't say that I always had rapt attention, but it made me feel good "scaffolding" the day for the kids and ourselves. I also kept at my seat two HUGE (think New York City telephone book, if they still print them) RV park guides and found our thrice-weekly next plug-in spot, then called (that's right, called—not clicked) ahead to reserve.

Did it work? Did we reconnect? Did we relax? Did we have FUN? A resounding YES to all of the above. I loved (just about) every minute. Mostly just the being together, but also the joy of watching Ben and Molly's sense of wonder at all we saw and experienced along the way: Molly and the parrot in Savannah, Ben and the Hip-Hop acrobats in New Orleans, fascination with the "brewing" process at Tabasco on Avery Island, the unanswered mysteries of AREA 51 in Roswell, the faces on Mount Rushmore lit one by one as the sun set, the

unequaled majesty of the Grand Canyon, and so much more. It's hard to say what stands out, but I cannot close without noting that it was the kids who asked if we could spend a couple extra days at Yellowstone—and when Ben told us that "Buffalo are really cool," right then I knew we had done a good thing.

Mary Herman
Brunswick, Maine

7

The Final Right Turn
Heading Home

Settling down meant a campfire and dinner under the stars. Here, I'm reading up on current events while Ben tends the fire. There was some discussion about who was the better fire builder. Ben prevailed by some quirk, the vote was 3 to 1—pesky democracy.

Oregon—The Coast, the Capital, and the Carousel

We got to Bandon (a couple hours from the California border, just south of Coos Bay) on a Friday afternoon and settled down to wait for Steve and Mary Ickes, who were coming down from Salem in their camper to meet us. Mary P. (Polacheck) and Mary H. (Herman) have been friends since they were babies in Milwaukee (that's babies, not babes—they're still babes).

Saturday was a big date for us—Ben's 13th birthday. A tradition in Mary's family is a birthday morning coffee cake with candles—served on an ancient rotating plate

Here, Ben looks down from Cape Arago, about twenty miles north of our campsite at a state park in Bandon.

The Oregon coast was something else—high green bluffs, jagged rocks, and constant surf.

Angus King 129

with a built-in music box that plays "Happy Birthday" sometimes and "Lullaby and Goodnight" other times. It's a little strange, but who am I to question family traditions?

We caravanned with the Ickes up to Salem on Sunday afternoon—Ben with me in the RV, Steve in their RV, and Molly with the two Marys in our car. This gave us a chance to try out our two-way radios between the three vehicles, and they worked slick. Steve acted as tour guide, pointing out the sights along the way (and there were lots); I supplied the bad jokes. The only bad moment was when the radio suddenly came to life and Steve said, "I know there's a tunnel up ahead, but I just can't remember how tall it is." My mind flashed back to the Merritt Parkway—way to make a bus driver nervous. But it turned out to be no problem.

On the way, we passed through Coos Bay (in Oregon, it's pronounced *Cooz,* as in Bob Cousy's nickname; in New Hampshire, it's *Cu-oz,* as in nothing else I can think of), Charleston, and Florence—all towns that bear a

How's this for the perfect water-fall? And here's Molly on the trail underneath it.

People back home have often asked about the beard; the thing to know is that I didn't intend to grow one. I just decided not to shave. A subtle difference, I realize, but important nonetheless.

Salem has the most wonderful carousel—not an antique, but brand new—with horses hand carved by local artists.

haunting resemblance to towns along the northeast coast of Maine. With once-thriving economies based on lumber and fishing, they now struggle to survive; the great mills are mostly silent and the boats few.

Tourism provides some relief, but it's seasonal, and the promise of high tech plays itself out in the more urban areas. It's hard to see the future of these towns, but I can't help believing that it's somehow wrapped up with the sea—as the ultimate amenity that will eventually attract the people whose presence will bring the jobs. This is already happening on the mid-Maine coast; I wish it would hurry up in Coos Bay and Eastport.

Once in Salem, we spent a day in Silver Falls State Park—a spectacular place about 45 minutes out of town. There are about a dozen waterfalls in the park, all along a beautiful set of well-maintained trails. It was almost like a rain forest—including trees completely covered by moss. It was really a neat place—Molly and I even saw a snake and a giant slug (I'll spare you the pictures, but I have them; Molly insisted).

Another stop in Oregon was at Nike in Beaverton. All the buildings in the amazing Nike complex (about 6,000 people work there) are named for famous athletes like Bo Jackson, Michael Jordan, and, of course, Maine's own Joan Benoit Samuelson.

And almost as spectacular as the Ahwahnee in Yosemite is the Timberline Lodge at the foot of Mt. Hood. Built in the mid-thirties as a WPA project, this is an extraordinary place. The workers were mostly local people who needed work during the Depression and they achieved an amazing blend of utilitarian architecture (it's a very comfortable ski lodge) and home-grown art. We wanted to come back.

Timberline Lodge is full of art, like these wonderful carvings, many done by people who were carpenters or laborers with no special training (except on the job).

Mary and Molly pose with Mary Seabright, who works at Nike and (you guessed it) is married to Mary's cousin Mark. See Olympian Joanie Benoit in the poster?

And this was a big (and hard) day; we put the RV on the market in anticipation of returning home in mid-June, using this picture in the ad. We'd have loved to keep it, but couldn't figure out when we'd use it. The kids had to get back to school, which only left summers to travel—and who wants to leave Maine in the summer?

Ain't she beautiful? And you should hear the SurroundSound.

On our way north to Washington, we took the stunning drive up the Columbia River Gorge and looped around Mt. Hood. As you can see, spring hasn't exactly overwhelmed the area—what a spectacular spot.

And so we said good-bye to Oregon, at the Wal-Mart parking lot where we spent the last night. Wal-Mart, as you may know, has a policy of letting RVers park overnight in their lots, which comes in real handy when you can't find a campground or it's too late to do all the setting-up. Naturally, we did some shopping (they have a great selection of RV supplies) as well; these guys didn't get to be the biggest store chain in the world by being stupid.

Then it was on to Washington and the third and final Right Turn. We even stopped at Mt. St. Helens; what a blast. Sorry, couldn't resist.

West of the Cascades—Flying Fish, a Timely Homer, and the Great Bed Race

Lest you think Mary is the only one with friends and relatives around the country, when we got to Seattle, we visited with my old friend from law school, Mike Fox, and his wife, Sally. (What if you're both a lawyer and a politician? Ouch.)

Mike and I both started in Legal Services right out of law school, in Washington and Maine, respectively. Mike made something of himself and is now a Superior Court Judge. I don't know where I went wrong.

And on a warm Sunday afternoon, what could be better than a ball game? We saw the Mariners beat the White Sox in a game that had

It's wonderful to be a member of a profession that is held in such high esteem wherever one goes; in this case, outside a bookstore in Seattle.

Here are Mike and Sally Fox and our gang about to get on one of the Puget Sound ferries. Seattle is like Portland (Maine) in this respect—a substantial number of people live on nearby islands and commute into the city by ferry. You'll notice that Fox looks considerably older than I do.

Ben smiled a lot, just not for the camera
—but I caught him here. Great kid.

Downtown Seattle from the top of the Space Needle; Puget Sound is to the right and Lake Washington is just out of the picture to the left. It's a beautiful city with a lot of life and energy.

A happy couple after the game. Notice the shadows—we had wonderful weather the whole time we were in Seattle. Maybe all this talk of rain is really to keep people from moving in, sort of the way we describe winter in Maine.

everything—homers, double plays, dropped fly balls (the sun was in his eyes; really), and a wonderful moment that usually only happens in the movies.

The most beloved Mariner of this era was Edgar Martinez—who had been with the team for eighteen years and was the designated hitter (I like it—what's the big deal about watching pitchers strike out? Mary, the baseball purist, hates it—it's the only thing she has in common with George Will.) Edgar was sort of the Yaz of the Mariners. Anyway, he was due to lead off the bottom of the 6th, and between innings they played a nice video tribute to him on the huge screen in center field. He came to the plate to a standing ovation, and, on the first pitch, hit it out. Pure Hollywood; the crowd, naturally, went nuts.

We had sun in Seattle and rain in San Diego. Go figure.

After the game, we had seafood on the wharf (you should see the size of the crabs out there—they're *huge)*.

And, of course, no visit to Seattle would be complete without a stop at the Pike Place Market. We wandered for a morning—fish (they throw them over the counter to be wrapped), antiques, restaurants, a store devoted entirely to left-handers (sample t-shirt: "If the right side of the brain controls the left side of the body, does that mean that only left-handers are in their right mind?"), magic tricks, luggage, collectibles (Wayne Gretzky's rookie card—$300), and old records and CDs. I bought the only album I've ever run across with not a single bad cut—Van Morrison's *Moondance.* Fabulous.

From Seattle, we headed north and west to the Olympic Peninsula and again experienced the contrast between our country's urban centers and the hinterlands. There were rolling fields, small towns, narrower roads, but

This was Mary's favorite spot in the beautiful town of Port Townsend, Washington. She and Molly are at the end of the counter—their third visit! It's a perfect 50s diner and even had a fully stocked jukebox (The Everly Brothers, The Coasters, Buddy Holly, The Big Bopper, Elvis, Bo Diddley, and the immortal Chuck Berry, among others).

Port Townsend is famous for its wonderfully preserved Victorian architecture—here are two examples downtown. How many towns in America would still look like this were it not for the well-meaning but ultimately disastrous urban renewal projects of the 50s and 60s? An old friend of mine once called urban renewal "the Federal Bulldozer."

...often the best stops were in places we never heard of.

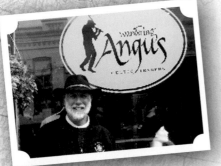

How can you not like a town with a store named "Wandering Angus"? This made me feel a little better after that rodents and politicians thing in Seattle.

Rhodys in bloom at the entrance to Fort Worden State Park.

lots going on, if you were to take the time to stop and look. One of our conclusions about the trip was that you can never really see America. There's just too much. On the other hand, no matter where you go—you could throw a dart at the map—you'll find nice people and cool stuff. We did a lot of thinking about spots we wanted to hit, but often the best stops were in places we never heard of (we didn't find too many people out there who'd heard of Brunswick, Maine, either)—all with their own character and stories. It's this sense of discovery and surprise that made the experience so special. Mary and I would do it again in a minute; the kids, maybe not.

We hit Port Townsend, Washington, not far from the westernmost point in the continental U.S., in the middle of the annual Rhody Fest (that's rhododendron, not helpers on a rock tour) and fell in love with the town. By the way, you know, of course, about the most famous married couple in the flower world, right? Phil and Rhoda Dendron, of course.

Our last look at the Pacific before heading east, toward home

We spent some time in the visitors center of the Olympic National Park, and drove to Hurricane Ridge for lunch. On the way into the lodge, we saw this encouraging sign.

Ben is helping Molly set up her own Yahoo! account at a cybercafe in Port Townsend. Look out, world, here she comes.

And Molly modeled a ranger hat; I'm not sure of the definition, but the word *insouciance* suggests itself for this expression.

Mom and Ben in a hot game of Mancala at a local coffee shop.

How's this for a prototype two-story RV? Yes, that's a 60s vintage VW Microbus welded on top.

We camped at Fort Worden State Park, just outside of Port Townsend, about a hundred yards from Puget Sound. This old army base was the setting for *An Officer and a Gentleman.* It was in great shape—and great demand; we had to leave Saturday morning because the RV park was completely booked that night. But at least we made the Friday nightbed races. Afterwards, we had a great meal in a local Thai restaurant. Who needs the city when you can have all this without the traffic?

On Thursday afternoon, Ben and I saw the premiere of *The Matrix: Reloaded* at The Rose Theatre, which was cool (the movie and the theater); maybe not up to the original, but cool all the same. Before the show, two local high-school kids took to the stage in front of the screen and did a *Matrix*-style fight, complete with a long black robe on the Neo character and slow-motion effects. It was surprising and great. When's the last time you saw a stage show before a movie at a Hoyts?

We spent a fair amount of time in the Cyber Bean Cafe, a friendly Inter-net coffee house (Moses was the always pleasant maître d'technology) with a fantastically fast connection. Buy a latte or smoothie and get ten

The Jefferson Transit District team heads to victory in the bed races.

The police pig bed didn't fare so well; perhaps because the cops were trying to run in helmets, combat boots, and flak vests. They were pretty good sports.

free minutes. I uploaded an Oregon update to our website in about a minute vs. the usual fifteen minutes with a regular dial-up connection in the RV park laundry room.

Finally, we spent a day in Olympic National Park, about fifty miles west of Port Townsend. Unfortunately, it was snowing most of the day and we missed some spectacular views.

East to Big Sky, the Wild West In Washington, Another Big Dam, and a River Running Through It.

We left western Washington on a Saturday (no room that night in the state park in Port Townsend because of the Rhody Fest) and made the third and final Big Right Turn of the trip. We were finally headed east, toward home, but with a whole continent to cross.

Our first stop after crossing the Cascades (which were beautiful, but challenging for the bus) was the improbable town of Winthrop, Washington. Improbable because it looked like an old-time western town, the kind you'd expect to find in Arizona, Texas, or in any one of a thousand movies about the old west. All false fronts and all in the old west style, right down to the wooden sidewalks.

Why, you could even ride broncos right there in front of the downtown ice cream parlor. Molly decided that a picture of herself in such an undignified pose wasn't in the cards. Mom wasn't so shy. (No, she doesn't like this photo of herself, but she did give me permission to use it.)

And what could be more appropriate in such a place than a cowboy from Maine? Remember the hat I ordered back in Fort Davis, Texas? Well, it finally caught up with us in Oregon, and here it is. You'll notice it in a lot more pictures to come; I slept in it the first three or four nights.

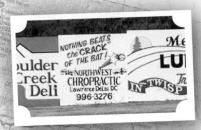

We loved this sign in the outfield—it's an ad for a local chiropractor and says, "Nothing Beats the CRACK of the Bat!"

All this and cable TV; who needs a city?

Ben and Jason immediately hit it off, as you can see from this picture of them trying to kill each other.

It sounds corny, but it worked. It could easily have been just another small town—a diner, a couple gas stations, and maybe a motel—the kind of place you roll right through. But its consistent style and fun shops made it impossible not to stop. So we did, and ended up staying three days. See why it's so important not to have a plan?

On the way through town, we came across a local softball game; the guys were about my age and older (if that's possible), and they played that each side got to bat ten men every inning. One of the players told me that it was "Canadian rules"; I'm still dubious.

In this area we discovered one of the most beautiful hotels we had ever seen anywhere, the Sun Mountain Lodge. We didn't get any pictures (Mary and I went there for dinner and forgot the camera), but it's a "don't miss" place if you're ever in this area. Perched on the top of a mountain, the hotel is a spa, hiking and horseback riding center in summer, and skiing destination in winter. Between the outstanding architecture and sensational views, it was a pretty special place.

Another reason we stuck around Winthrop for longer than we expected was a really nice RV park right on the river (River Bend RV Park), run by nice people who had a son just about Ben's age. The one drawback of a trip like this is that the kids are stuck with each other and (horrors) their parents for companionship, 24/7.

From Central Washington, we continued east through Spokane, where Mary found the very house where her parents lived in 1942, while her dad was in basic training for the Army Air Corps.

On the way, we had a quick stop at the Grand Coulee Dam, which, while not as dramatic as Hoover, is nonetheless an amazing sight. The best part was a film (narrated by Mainer Jack Perkins) on the history and politics of the project and what it brought to the Northwest in the way of flood control, power, and irrigation. Any bets on whether it could be built today?

Our next stop was Missoula, Montana, where we stayed at (yep, you guessed it) another fun RV park, this one based upon the "Jellystone" theme, complete with a giant statue of Yogi Bear.

And then we reached Channels Ranch, one of the long-fixed destinations of the trip. Channels is located in Ennis, Montana, and is owned by a group of fly-fishing enthusiasts, mostly from Texas. It's managed by Bill and Connie Owen, and Connie, like Mary Ickes in Oregon, grew up with Mary in Milwaukee, from age one through high school.

And what would a visit to Jellystone be without a picture with Yogi? Molly was a little reluctant; maybe she's afraid this will show up on a bulletin board at her wedding. And it just might.

Mary at Jellystone Park—it's actually one of a chain, mostly in the Midwest—at which we played miniature golf and the nicest restrooms and showers, bar none. (Hey, these things are important.)

An old friend of Mary's from Calais, John Haven, and my new friend Russ Fletcher, both of whom live in the Missoula area.

Now, it wouldn't be quite honest to leave you with the image above; I'm not that good a fly-caster and spent considerable time untangling. Maybe it was the hat.

What a place. On one side was the Madison River and Ennis Lake; on the other, hills rising to snow-capped mountains. The kids loved it (we'd still be there if Ben had his way); horses, dogs, cows, and incredible space.

To be on the Madison and not go fly fishing would be like visiting Maine and skipping the coast. It is, quite simply, the most famous fly-fishing river in America, if not the world. So while the kids, Mary, and Connie went on a trail ride into the mountains (where they saw a bear), Bill and I floated the river. We didn't have much luck (at this time of year, the runoff muddies the water), but managed to hook a few and certainly had a great time. A bad day fishing still beats a good day at most anything else.

Here's the Madison, flowing north (I can't get used to rivers flowing north) to meet the Jefferson and the Gallatin rivers in the town of (what else?) Three Forks. This is the headwaters of the Missouri River and the place where Lewis and Clark had to start walking.

This is Mammoth Hot Springs Village, looking northeast from the top of the springs in Yellowstone. We left the RV up on I-90 (I wasn't sure about the roads in the park—they turned out to be no problem), and stayed in one of the 1930s vintage cabin.

Here's a fun shot of the interior of our cabin at Yellowstone. The cabins weren't exactly luxurious, but were clean and comfortable. It was a great place, and the price (about $60 a night) was right.

Yellowstone—The Difference Between Buffalo and Bison

In its variety, size, geology, wildlife, and sheer beauty, there is nothing to rival Yellowstone National Park. We were overwhelmed. It is magnificent in every sense of the word.

And the best part is that there is so much to see and do in so many different locations that it doesn't have the crowded feeling of Yosemite and the Grand Canyon. In a sense, there are at least five different parks—the hot springs at the northern end, Old Faithful in the middle, Yellowstone Lake, the Canyon to the east, and wildlife all over the place. It was the wildlife that really woke up the kids when we entered the park. After hours of canyons and forests, they had become pretty jaded about views—but when a herd of bison ambled in front of the car, they were re-energized and hooked on sightings.

The thing to understand about Yellowstone is that it's one of the most volcanically active areas in the world. It was the site of the largest volcanic

Here's the granddaddy of geysers—Old Faithful, in full eruption. We learned to our disappointment that it doesn't really go off on the hour, or even hourly. It actually goes off every ninety minutes or so, but when it does, it's worth the wait.

This is one of the hundreds (maybe thousands) of thermal pools scattered throughout the park. There were full-blown geysers, bubbling mud springs, multicolored seeping hot springs (they really were hot; I stuck my finger in), and everything in between.

Two girls by a hot pool; think Mary was nervous with Molly this high up on the fence?

Molly at the edge of one of the hot springs. I was surprised at how dynamic this all is; not far from this spot, we saw deposits forming on fresh grass.

Almost as much fun as watching the eruption is watching the people watching the eruption.

The interior of the Old Faithful Inn is one of the most spectacular interior spaces in the country—six stories open to the top around a massive stone fireplace. The tree knees were picked one-by-one by the architect to match; the lights, the floors, the window trim, even the writing desks on the mezzanine, all fit together in a great grand lodge style.

All the states have nicknames, but few are as appropriate as Montana's (the Big Sky State)—the sky really was bigger, deeper, and bluer than any place I'd ever seen. Here, in the valley of the Madison River, it seems to go on forever.

We actually saw O.F. go off three times—twice from the ground and here from the balcony of the Old Faithful Inn. (Hint: Buy lunch at the snack bar downstairs and bring it up to the porch to wait for the next show.)

Yellowstone National Parks lower falls taken from Artist Point.

eruption in the history of the planet 35 million years ago, and a pretty sizable one only 600,000 years ago. Ben and I kept looking at each other and saying, "And we're going to sleep in this place tonight? It could blow any minute."

Ten years from now, it could look entirely different. Or, it could all be gone in a big bang. Think Old Man of the Mountain.

I never knew it, but Yellowstone has its own Grand Canyon—better than a thousand feet deep, with several dramatic falls and breathtaking views into the gorge.

As we looked down, however, I realized that as far as canyons went, we had done the trip backwards. We should have started with the Badlands in South Dakota, done Bryce, Arches, Canyonlands, and Yellowstone (in pretty much any order), but ended up at the ("Original") Grand Canyon.

A bend in the Yellowstone River as it approaches the gorge. It would be a great place to kayak—until you hit the 150-foot drop about a quarter mile below this spot.

A nice shot of Yellowstone Lake, taken from the car by Mary.

And finally, the animals. As I mentioned, even our somewhat jaded kids came to life when we came across sights like these. Some of our best moments came as we drove through the park at the end of the day.

Here is a climber on his way up Devils Tower. As Ben and I walked around the base, we saw probably a dozen men and women making the ascent. Not my choice for a free-time activity, but this guy probably thinks politics ain't so smart, either.

The Grand Canyon is so huge, beautiful, and completely awe-inspiring, that anything you see later just doesn't measure up. I kept feeling a little let down, sort of like visiting New Hampshire or Vermont after you've been to Maine.

My zoom isn't all that great; we had to be pretty close to get good shots of animals (taken by Ben, by the way—he seems to have evolved into our wildlife photographer). Another night, we saw a grizzly (dimly, to be sure) hunting in the midst of a group of buffalo.

Yellowstone was the first national park established anywhere in the world, and what a wonderful precedent it set—accessible, yet largely unspoiled, it is one of our country's gems. I believe setting aside places like this is one of the most far-seeing and important things one generation can do for another; we are blessed to have it in our midst. As Ken Burns has said, the national parks are one of America's best ideas.

The Tower looks like a huge tree stump (which is what it is in the local Indian legend) and you can see why it's tough for someone into technical rock climbing to resist.

Heading Home—The Badlands, The B-1, and the A-Maize-ing Corn Palace

On the way, sort of, from Yellowstone to the Black Hills is Devil's Tower, famous as a destination for rock climbers and alien spaceships. It's a dramatic formation, made all the more so by the fact that it rises virtually alone from the floor of the plateau. (Remember Richard Dreyfus playing the cosmic Whirlitzer on this spot? The year, believe it or not, was 1978.)

After Devil's Tower, we had one more scheduled stop—in western South Dakota—to see Mount Rushmore, the Badlands, and our friends David and Jayne Hickey, who live just outside Rapid City. Jayne is the daughter of one of Mary's best friends growing up in Milwaukee and worked for us for a time in the early 80s as a babysitter for the big boys (who were 32, 30, and 27 at the time of this trip and needed very little, if any, baby-sitting). David is from South Gardiner, Maine, and was a "Wizzo" on a B-1 bomber for the U.S. Air Force. "Wizzo" is short for "Weapons Systems Officer," the guy who's in charge of dropping the precision-guided bombs and evasive action if the plane is attacked.

David had just returned from Iraq, where he had flown both the first and last missions of his squadron's deployment. He gave us a tour of his plane, but I didn't take any pictures for fear of breaching a security rule (a very nice young man and woman let us onto the tarmac, but they were carrying some serious automatic weapons; I was on my best behavior). Take my word for it, the plane was all business—very small cockpit (about the size of a Ford Explorer for four—two pilots and two Wizzos); everything else was bomb bays.

The Hickeys' house was at Ellsworth Air Force Base, just east of Rapid City. It was a perfect stopover for us because not only did we get a great visit with our friends, but also it was near Mount Rushmore, the Crazy Horse Monument, and Badlands National Park.

Ben, Kyle, David, and I had some good touch football (the old guys were all-time quarterbacks while the kids ran themselves into the ground); the final score was 36-36. David told me that when he played for Gardiner, they never lost to Cony.

We did enjoy a real family activity outside of Rapid City, however—a night at the Flying T Ranch—with

Mary gives a lesson in the ancient art of cat's cradle to the Hickeys' daughter, Emma. Molly and Emma became fast friends, as did Ben and their son Kyle.

Molly reading in the passenger seat on the road through South Dakota.

And here are the presidents on their mountain, about fifteen miles from Crazy Horse. This is one of those places (like the Grand Canyon or the Montana sky) that simply can't be captured in any picture.

chuck wagon food, surprisingly good western music, and ancient vaudeville-type humor, which consisted mostly of North Dakota jokes, which seemed to be big around there. I, myself, would never make fun of New Hampshire. Except sometimes.

And then came the Badlands, an amazing combination of gullies, canyons, striated rock formations, and wide-open prairie. We took a great loop right off the Interstate that wound through a good deal of the park.

One minute we were in flat grasslands that seemed to go on for miles, and then, suddenly, we were down into a maze-like set of canyons. It was much smaller than the Grand Canyon, but we did have the experience of driving down into and through it. We didn't stay long, but it was sure worth the detour.

Our final stop in South Dakota was the famous Corn Palace in the town of Mitchell. Essentially, it was a big auditorium/gym covered with corn. Literally. Red corn, yellow corn, brown corn, corn stalks, corn ears, corn kernels, corn leaves.

Virtually everything you see in this picture (except Mom and Molly) is made of corn—and they change the pictures every year.

Here's how they do it: sort of like a big corn-by-number set. Each one of those little bricks is half an ear of corn.

At about the time we were heading to Mt. Rushmore, we listened to a book-on-tape of *Timeline* by Michael Crichton. Without giving too much away, one of its themes had the bad guys creating super tourist attractions, which they would generously give to the public while quietly buying up all the surrounding real estate to profit from the spin-off business. And lo and behold, here it is, in real life. See Washington at the top?

By this point, we were truly on the way home, with few stops except to sleep—from South Dakota up through Minnesota to Duluth, across the top of Wisconsin and the Upper Peninsula of Michigan to Sault Ste. Marie, then into Canada, and from there, home to Maine.

It was hard to believe that it was almost over—our rolling, rollicking, sometimes (but only sometimes) rocky joyride across America. We had seen only a small part of all there is to see and met only a few of the millions of people out there. But at least we tried—to make America real to ourselves and the kids, to see what family means when all you have is each other, to experience the mystical bonds of place and time that hold us all together.

Going Home—Minnesota, Michigan, Canada, and Home to Maine

South Dakota was our last scheduled stopping place. From there, it was almost due east—diagonally up through Minnesota, across the top of Wisconsin, and on to the Upper Peninsula of Michigan. At Sault Ste. Marie, we crossed into Ontario and were on the last leg toward northern New England.

At least there's no pretense of this being a family activity. The West is unfortunately full of these so-called casinos. How could anybody argue that this would be good for Maine?

And speaking of enterprise, how about this juxtaposition in downtown Rapid City? Just get an advance on your paycheck and go right next door and lose it at video poker.

One of our final stops was at a small RV park in Ontario, which was quite a social place. When darkness fell, campfires sprang up across the park and neighbors gathered for gentle conversation. It was the kind of socializing we had hoped to find all along the trip, but largely missed because the consistently cool weather often kept everyone (including us) inside.

One of the reasons we took the Canadian route home (the other was to avoid the traffic around Chicago) was to stop for a couple days at Mary's cabin near Algonquin Provincial Park in Ontario. She bought the land in the early 70s ($900 for a lakeside acre) and she and her brothers and assorted friends (I wasn't in the picture then) built this classic northwoods cabin.

One of the neat things about the way they developed the lake is that all the building lots are on the same side--so you have neighbors on either side but the view across the lake is of a pristine lake shore. I'd never seen this anywhere else, but it makes a lot of sense, both for the ecology of the lake and the owners.

It's a wonderful spot; we just wish it wasn't fourteen hours from Maine.

The kids enjoyed a break from driving.

I did a little lifeguarding; no way I was getting in that cold water except in the case of dire emergency.

Molly with Jack Hurley. At the end of the day, it's a special gift to be able to pick up and hold something of such beauty that your hands have made.

Back in the RV, Ben plays Star Wars (thanks, George) on two computers at once. Actually, the computer on the left has a broken screen so it's hooked up to the screen on the right. His left hand is running the keyboard and he handles the mouse with his right while focusing on the screen in the middle. No wonder these kids make great fighter pilots.

Here's a beautiful sunset just east of the Sault; the RV park we discovered was almost full of what I would call permanent campers—small trailers that stay for the whole summer serving as low-cost cottages for folks from all over Ontario.

That night in the cabin, we made a fire, read Agatha Christie, and listened to the rain on the roof; does it get any better?

Another treat was an afternoon visit with Jack Hurley, an old friend of Mary and her brothers, who makes the most beautiful canoes you ever saw. Jack came to summer camp in Algonquin Provincial Park in the 60s and, for all intents and purposes, never left. Now he's one of a handful (more than a few of whom are in Maine) dedicated to the art of the wood and canvas canoe. Years later, Ben even made one himself—and its a beauty.

Jack and his associate build—completely by hand—about fifteen canoes a year, along with maintaining and rebuilding a dozen or so more. In his

Finally, back into Maine over Route 2 to Bethel, then down 26 to Norway-South Paris and 121 to Auburn. Here we are, headed for the Androscoggin and 196 to Topsham. At this point, the kids asked, "how much longer" about every two minutes.

Isn't this just a perfect Vermont shot? We're on I-91 headed for St. Johnsbury and the final run to Maine. This was a welcome sight after a really awful drive through the construction and generally horrendous traffic around Montreal.

The Topsham-Brunswick bridge; now we really were five minutes from home.

After five-and-a-half months, 33 states, and fifteen thousand miles, we were home. The neighborhood kids formed a welcoming party and we managed to get the Dutch Star under the wires and into the dooryard.

shop, I felt like I was in a kind of zen space where concepts like art, quality, integrity, and honesty find concrete form. It was really cool, especially to someone (like me) whose career has been mostly taken up with abstractions such as law or policy.

Did you ever wonder what you would do if you were driving through Renfrew, Ontario, around noon and everybody wanted to stop for lunch? Answer—just pull up to one side of Main Street, take up four parking spaces, and have a leisurely lunch at a sidewalk cafe. Believe it not, I put quarters in all four parking meters. This turned out to have been a good move—about ten minutes later, so help me, the meter maid came by and dutifully checked each one. Honesty is the best policy.

This is what we saw as we made the turn into the driveway; pretty neat.

And here they are—just about all the neighborhood kids. The hardest part of the trip for Ben and Molly was the lack of companionship. Sure, they had each other and us and made some friends along the way, but they still missed their buddies.

And this is the scene fifteen minutes later in our backyard. It reminded me of the great children's book about the guy who sells hats that are stolen by a bunch of monkeys; here they are, all up a tree. This is fun itself.

The main reason we pushed so hard to be home by mid-June was so the kids could have a few days to rejoin their classmates before school closed for the summer. And sure enough, here we are in Molly's third-grade class, putting the finishing touches on a wonderful map they had made to chart our progress around the country.

And finally, we were back in Maine, headed for Brunswick from the west.

It sure felt good to see so many familiar landmarks.

I also had a "former Governor" moment when we hit the Maine border and Route 2 (which had been pretty good through New Hampshire) turned patched and bumpy. I was crestfallen until Mary reminded me that it was no longer my problem. In the old days, I'd have called the DOT and raised hell (just ask 'em).

In a larger sense, our little crew will never be fully home; while we started out to take the trip, in the end, the trip took us. All we saw, learned, experienced, and came to know about this wonderful country—and each other—is now inextricably bound into our lives.

And on top of all that, we sure did have fun along the way; thanks so much for joining us!

With love and safe travels to all,

Ben, Molly, Mary, and Angus

Epilogue

When I was in college, I got a simple piece of advice from an old New Hampshire man that literally changed my life—and had a lot to do with our trip.

"When you get to be my age," he wheezed, "you're going to regret things about your life; see that you regret the things that you did, rather than the things you didn't do."

Wow. What a profound observation. Err on the side of action.

I have found that it's always easier to summon a list of arguments against any particular course of action, especially if that action involves any change from the routine or expected. Start a brand new business (with a totally new business model) when you're 45, out of work, have a kid in college, and two more coming along? The question practically answers itself; fortunately, remembering the advice of the old man, I decided to give it a try. By the same token, how about this one—does it make sense to run for governor when you've never

... regret the things that you did, rather than the things you didn't do.

even run for dogcatcher, have no affiliation to a political party, no organization, no staff, and somewhere in the neighborhood of 10% name recognition?

In the latter case, the final decision was explicitly based upon the old man's advice, this time via my teenage son, Duncan. After a long family discussion on the pros and cons of entering the race (with something like fourteen other candidates), Duncan piped up, "Dad, you've got to do it; what if you don't even try and Maine falls further behind; you'll never forgive yourself." And that was it; I was in.

So it was with this trip—there were lots of reasons not to go: expense, taking the kids out of school, gross inexperience in piloting a bus, uncertain itinerary, possible (likely?) family friction, weird looks from my friends. But the idea of trying it, of seeing America firsthand, was just too strong.

And it was one of the best decisions I ever made.

After re-reading the above, I realized that I used the word "I" five times; eight if you count the three in this sentence. This is a mistake and leads me to another important point about the trip: Mary was absolutely at the center of the whole deal; you just couldn't undertake something like this without a willing and enthusiastic partner. This goes way beyond the practical stuff like arranging the kids' home-schooling certification from the state, checking the guidebooks along the way, thinking about groceries and clean clothes, or doing most of the navigation. Her really important contribution was her enthusiasm for what we were seeing and experiencing, her unfailing good cheer, and her positive support for the whole idea. It's hard to put into words how important this is. I never a moment felt that she was just being dragged along or that she was humoring me or doing some kind of wifely duty. She didn't just go along, she aided and abetted—and that gave the whole experience a fun, positive tone.

And now she's the one egging me on to do it again when Molly is up and out.

Which brings us back full circle. I'm convinced that we are the hardest working, most scheduled and regimented people in history. So regimented, in fact, that we often don't notice life when it stares us in the face; and we certainly don't celebrate enough. Even at the best of moments—a child's wedding, a promotion, the birth of a grandchild—we are programmed to worry about something just around the corner.

When I was in my twenties, I took another great trip—a summer tour of Europe by motorcycle with some friends. We soon learned that traveling in a strange country on a motorcycle was no fun in the rain (and was often downright dangerous). The reality, of course, was that it didn't rain all the time or even much of the time, but we noticed after driving through the first few storms that even on the clearest day, a tiny cloud on the horizon would awaken a nagging anxiety—and compromise the exhilaration that should have been ours.

I have never been able to fully shake this, but haven't given up trying. One instant remedy is to take a deep breath, to literally slow down—and in many ways, that was exactly the point of the trip, and it worked. In fact, it was the longest, deepest breath I ever drew, and boy was it worth it. ◈